The Fire and the Rose: The Wedding of Spirituality and Sexuality is a powerful, sensitive, loving, personal, and understandable depth plunge into the two most misunderstood and abused topics of our day. Anyone honest enough to admit struggling with spirituality and sexuality in our day would benefit greatly from this excellent work and its practical suggestions. It is not a "fix it" work with easy answers, but rather ideas to challenge, teach, and point directions toward becoming transformed.

> G. Keith Parker, Ph.D.
> Jungian analyst and pastoral counselor,
> author of *Seven Cherokee Myths*

An admirer of Bud Harris's *Sacred Selfishness*, I have read his new work, *The Fire and the Rose*, three times now and find something fresh and necessary to my life in each reading. Dr. Harris is generous with his personal history, widely read, and deeply involved in the human journey. He is a healer in words and stories.

> Gail Godwin, Ph.D.
> Novelist and author of *Father Melancholy's Daughter* and *Evensong*

Bud Harris as spiritual guide suggests that when life becomes stagnant and congealed, most often sexuality brings a new crisis fraught with the high cost and great promise of the fire of the numinous. The desire that seems to be wrecking our lives may well be the Self awakening us to Soul and the Divine. Such uncomfortable and disturbing occasions at any age open us to a frightening and elusive link between the sensual and the spiritual. The choice, Harris proposes, is dead soul, addiction, or discovering those questions that keep us alive and thirsty.

> Reverend Dr. Bill Dols
> Creator and editor of the *Bible Workbench*,
> co-author of *Finding Jesus, Discovering Self: Passages to Healing and Wholeness*

A deeply soulful book written from the heart, filled with wisdom, intimate personal sharing, challenging questions, and insights into the wonders and mysteries of sexuality and spirituality. This book is significant for all of us, and a timely resource for psychotherapists and spiritual directors. Bud is a master teacher, the perfect guide for the journey of living an authentic life. I can't wait to share this book with others, especially my clients.

Gail Vaughn Rogers, M.A.
Psychotherapist, retreat leader,
associate editor of the *Bible Workbench*

Dr. Bud Harris, Jungian analyst and writer, has covered the topic of sexuality, love, inner conflict, and transformation in his readable and personal book, *The Fire and the Rose*. Quoting Eleanor Roosevelt, Dostoevsky, Rilke, Gail Godwin, and Jung, among many others, he explores with humility and wisdom the tension spirituality and sexuality bring to individuals, couples, and societies. Without declaring easy answers, Dr. Harris reminds one of the complexity of the psyche, the need to continue to live with rather than fix suffering, and the *numinosity tremendum* of our journey toward a paradoxical, unique life. He has added points of discussion at the end of several chapters as well as helpful guidelines in dealing with dreams. Buried in Dr. Harris's conclusion are four points of truth he has discovered along his way—they are indisputable, substantial, and alone worth the read. I highly recommend this book.

Tess Castleman, M.A., L.P.C.
Jungian analyst, author of *Threads, Knots, Tapestries*

Our ancestors considered Eros a god; Jung once defined a neurosis as "a neglected god." In *The Fire and the Rose*, Bud Harris addresses this neurotic split between divinity and the body, between spirit and matter, and proffers a path of reconciliation and reclamation of sexuality as a vital link to a fuller expression of spirit. Full of personal confession, case examples, and exercises, this work offers both theoretic and practical tips to personal and cultural healings.

James Hollis, Ph.D.
Jungian analyst, author of *Finding Meaning in the Second Half of Life*

Bud Harris generously shares how his deepest early wound began a struggle to redefine perceptions of God and to make tough choices about money, vocation, family, and authentic relationship to Self and community.

Bud sees *spirituality* as the driving force that moves us into a life connected to something greater than ourselves and *desire* as awakening the soul, ridding us of fear, and nourishing us during our lifelong journey "of becoming." He encourages us to question the contradictions in our lives and to expand the questions beyond what is safe and secure.

Always accessible to the reader, Harris uses examples from fairy tales to show that often "doing the wrong things transforms life for the better." His candid recounting of personal challenges and those of his clients help us define what it is to be human . . . all the wrong decisions we make and the courage it takes to change. He suggests solutions: to journal, to record nighttime dreams, and to understand metaphor in religion, literature, and myth as a source of wisdom. He challenges us to create joyful, passionate, and meaningful lives leading to repeated transformation.

Charlotte M. Mathes, Ph.D.
Jungian analyst, author of *And a Sword Shall Pierce Your Heart*

This book is studded with examples of healing junctures at which the soul's desire for wholeness breaks through and turns out to be decisive in the battle to live more fully, more ethically, and more forcefully. Bud Harris uncovers private desires that often go unspoken for by the depth psychologists, even though they hear about them daily in the dreams and situations that drive individuals into therapy. Although this Jungian analyst recognizes the paradoxical sacredness of the desire to break any preestablished mold for the soul, his is not a book filled with prescriptions to abandon the constraints of the moral sense to the pleasures of wholeness. Rather, he invites the reader to meander in the labyrinth of the Self and there to engage with one's particular monster. His wise counsel, to live the paradox of freedom through honest engagement with the shadow, is the Ariadne thread of a mature *anima*. Those who are willing to peruse these pages with the same care their author has brought to writing them will have a safe enough journey—not perhaps into heroic mastery, but certainly into the embrace of life itself.

John Beebe, M.D.
Jungian analyst, author of *Integrity in Depth*

THE FIRE AND THE ROSE

Also by Bud Harris

Sacred Selfishness: A Guide to Living a Life of Substance

The Father Quest: Rediscovering an Elemental Psychic Force

Emasculation of the Unicorn: The Loss and Rebuilding of Masculinity in America

co-authored with Massimilla Harris

Like Gold Through Fire: Understanding the Transforming Power of Suffering

THE
FIRE
AND
THE
ROSE

The Wedding of Spirituality and Sexuality

BUD HARRIS, PH.D.

CHIRON PUBLICATIONS • WILMETTE, ILLINOIS

Library of Congress Cataloging-in-Publication Data

Harris, Clifton Tumlin Bud, 1937–
The fire and the rose : the wedding of spirituality and sexuality / Bud Harris.
p. cm.
Includes bibliographical references and index.
ISBN 978-1-888602-42-5 (alk. paper)
1. Self-actualization (Psychology) 2. Jungian psychology. 3. Spirituality. 4. Sex. I. Title.

BF637.S4H36 2007
155.3'2—dc22   2007010503

We shall not cease from exploration
And the end of all our exploring
Will be to arrive where we started
And know the place for the first time.
And all shall be well and
All manner of thing shall be well
When the tongues of flame are in-folded
Into the crowned knot of fire
And the fire and the rose are one.

—T. S. ELIOT, *FOUR QUARTETS*, "LITTLE
GIDDING"

Contents

Acknowledgments

This book is the product of many years of reflections on my plunge through life. Always present in my mind are Massimilla, Cliff, Marjorie, Betsy, Galen, and Ben. Father and mother, Bud senior and Marjorie, pulse in my blood. A special thanks must go to the men, women, and children whom I've been privileged to know and work with in my professional life. I want to assure them all, who have labored to understand themselves and to grow through life's challenges, that the stories in this book are fictionalized compositions. They have emerged from my thirty plus years of experience and while representative of real-life experiences, they are not based on any particular person's story.

Susan Gabriel was a treasure, as she has been for over a decade, in helping me bring the manuscript together. Susan Leon made many valuable contributions. Kirsten Whatley graciously challenged and guided me to stretch beyond my limits again and again. Siobhan Drummond, the project manager for this book at Chiron, has deftly steered this manuscript into a book. My copy editor, Sara Gallogly's ability to combine precision with insight quickly gained my appreciation and made our work together a pleasure. The team at Chiron has shown the kind of creativity and helpfulness that make turning a manuscript into a book exciting and fun.

Over the years many people have contributed to the development and refinement of my writing efforts and provided abundant encouragement. I wish to thank them all. Among them are Gail Godwin, Karyla Gaines, Dale Sargent, Sim Cozart, and Lynn Brannon Magino.

Introduction

Who then devised this torment? Love.
Love is the unfamiliar Name
Behind the hands that wove
The intolerable shirt of flame
Which human power cannot remove.
We only live, only suspire
Consumed by either fire or fire.

—T. S. ELIOT, *FOUR QUARTETS*, "LITTLE GIDDING"

There was a time in my life when I walked through the world as a confident, self-controlled man. My self-control was part of the way I defined myself and certainly the part I most respected. Yet it enabled me to grow up a stranger to myself, so that only with the life-changing experiences that began the journey I now refer to as my destiny did I begin to think about what desire really means. I gradually realized that beneath the facade of my self-definition there were deeper stirrings that moved with a tidal force. What I have learned is that desire, whether it is for another person, for material objects, or for the Divine, is a hunger to participate in life on a more intense level than we can achieve on our own. Ultimately, I believe desire must be for participation and not for possession, or we will end up destroying the experience we are seeking. In its fullest sense desire is a longing to involve ourselves in the spirit and the body of the world. Through the body, which means through our senses, feelings and thoughts, desire pours itself into our experiences. Through self-awareness and reflection we are able to open our heart's deepest secrets, allow our desire to become creative, and make life richer and increasingly meaningful.

Desire gives birth to passion, which, if we are timid, often wears the disguise of fear, disparagement, or even envy and resentment. Passion is both a longing for and a feeling of being compelled toward someone or something outside of ourselves. Passion arouses us to action, fills us with enthusiasm and overcomes the fear of suffering in the pursuit of our desire. Desire and longing go together like identical twins. And in many cases, the object of our fierce desire may also be reflecting a secret yearning for something unrealized deep within our own makeup.

Conventional wisdom fears passion because it may thrust us blindly out of the pinched shoes of propriety and the roles we've been shoehorned into by family and society, and into the chaos of ecstasy or despair. Whether recognized or not, passion fuels the divine courses of our sexuality and spirituality until either they come together in a blossoming tree of fire or we shrink back into the safety of provisional lives.

Making the complexity of our lives clear and understandable is a challenge whenever one tries to write about one's experience. I use my own story and the fictionalized versions of people I've worked with to illustrate many of the points I'm writing about. In addition, I use material from classic literature and religious traditions to show how the challenges of life combine against us and yet contain the answers we are seeking. These stories remind us, in ways that our television shows and movies rarely do, that our struggles, failures and suffering have a place in the progression of meaning and fulfillment in our lives. Therefore, I am trying to avoid the common mistake of many self-help books, which is to see life in simplistic terms. As a practicing analyst I learned many years ago that to try to deny the complexity of being human leads to living frustrated and disappointed lives.

Life at its best is never a spectator sport. Once we are adults, spiritual and psychological growth is always a choice that must be backed up with committed efforts. In my previous book, *Sacred Selfishness*, I devoted part two of the book to methods of exploring ourselves and our lives. These methods—journaling, befriending dreams, and dialoguing—have become my spiritual practices.

I call them that because I have learned that if I do them religiously they will transform my life. At the end of each part in this book I will give you a few questions that can help you explore my themes in the context of your life and invite transformation to begin. I also suggest that you pay attention to your dreams while you are reading and reflecting on these questions and include them in your journal. There are a few tips on journaling and dreamwork in the appendix.

This book continues the journey I began in *Sacred Selfishness* into the vision of love as the foundation of a satisfying life. To try and make love simple, sweet and comforting is to ignore the stormy reality of life. The same reality is true for spirituality and sexuality. Our encounters with love, spirituality and sexuality have played a major role in shaping who we are. This reality alone makes it worth our while to understand how these experiences have affected us. However, our wish to feel more vitality, happiness and fulfillment may also lead us to explore both the animation and the pain these forces can bring to us. If we search thoughtfully we can also discover the promise of how these potent parts of our lives energize us and are woven into the pattern of wholeness representing our potential. Though a book like this one cannot be naively reassuring, I hope you will find it stimulating and inspiring. As I have written it I have kept in mind the requests of many readers to share more of my own journey and I am honored if we become fellow travelers.

* * *

For over thirty years I have worked with people who want to find passion in their lives, who want to believe in love, no matter how bitter, betrayed or cynical they may feel. They yearn to feel the presence of the Divine or some spiritual structure in their lives that brings a sense of meaning to daily existence beyond the practicality of our social values. They long for the word *soul* to have a personal meaning. During the darkest hours of our work together we learned that life thrives and renews itself on new insights and understandings, fresh self-awareness and increasing inner integrity.

I am writing to honor these people and in an effort to share what we've learned in a way that can strengthen others who are on a similar quest. The quest includes those who are spiritually seeking, those who are trying to face themselves more honestly, and those who want a more complete experience of life's meaning.

As soon as I began to write this manuscript I realized that I had been working on this project since adolescence—that time when I began to burn with sexuality and was crushed by the failure of my religious beliefs. These events seized me unawares, and I have often felt like Alice, moving confidently and naively through life until I'd fall into some unseen rabbit hole, into a new topsy-turvy world. Initially, such a plunge would leave me tempted to scurry back to the values of my childhood and the parents and teachers I saw as powerful. But I've long since learned that, as safe and secure as the old ways appear, they can easily become a tomb for the spirit. When coupled with practicality and busyness, they can dampen the fires of passionate longings and force the potency of love underground. What I have learned is that by reflecting upon the events of my life, I am able to find a pattern in them and the lessons they contain for me.

The Swiss psychiatrist Carl Jung warned us that when we lose the aptitude for love it is replaced by the need for power. He noted that fire sleeps even in the dead ashes of our hearts and then re-kindles in the darker areas of our lives if it has no other place to go. If we can't awaken to our spiritual and sexual fire then it usually finds other outlets. Our fire may appear in disguise as emotional symptoms of distress or as excesses such as fundamentalism, addictions, compulsive sexuality, overly busy lives and other problems that erode our existence spiritually and physically.

Desire and passion are the fire that makes up "the shirt of flame" in the poem at the beginning of this introduction. The "rose," another of the famous poetic images used by T. S. Eliot, is surely love. If we are going to be fully alive, our task is to seek to understand these fountainheads of life. This work becomes as joyful as it is painful when its focus is to transform ourselves until we become the container of wholeness in which the fire and the rose are one.

Another set of desires lives deep within us as well. We can cope with life, manage our affairs and be successful in a conventional way, and still we may experience a mysterious longing. It is a longing to know if we can have faith in reality, in the truth of our existence, so that our lives will have purpose, meaning and a way of being fulfilled. These are the longings of the soul. The word *soul* in Jungian psychology is not the same word I heard during my Protestant boyhood, nor is it the same word so easily tossed around in New Age circles. It is the translation of the Greek word *psyche* that Jungians have used for decades. It speaks of the mystery and depth that is part of our being that we often intuit.

Our soul carries the powerful desire to live a life that is serving something greater than ourselves and is advancing the cause of meaning in our lives. It makes us most profoundly human and at the same time connects us to the great mystery of life. When we pay attention to our inner life, bringing our conscious selves into relationship with matters of the heart and the expressions of the unconscious, we are paying attention to our soul. When we ask the meaning of a feeling or a mood, reflect upon our experiences, question a physical symptom, ponder a dream or dialogue with part of ourselves, we are relating to our soul. And, when life is stretching us farther than we want to be stretched, forcing us to grow and give up comfortable old patterns, it is our soul at work. We become the container for "the fire," desire, and "the rose," love, as we grow toward wholeness in relationship to our soul.

* * *

The language of Jungian psychology can also help us understand the complexity of our experiences. For example, the term *Self* designates an important part of our personality that is in service to the soul. Jungians capitalize it to separate it from our everyday or ego "selves" and use it to describe the archetypal image of a person's fullest potential and the unity of the personality as a whole. Psychologically, it is thought of as the unifying principle within our personality and therefore represents the central position of author-

THE FIRE AND THE ROSE

ity in relation to our psychological life and personal destiny. In its service to the soul, the Self uses desire as one of its primary tools to lure or push us toward wholeness or to crack the shell of a rigidified life. I will discuss the Self in more detail as an image of the Divine demanding to be recognized in each of us. In the Western tradition it is often referred to as the "image of God" within us. In the Buddhist tradition it might be a metaphor for enlightenment or "Buddha consciousness." Many of the great religions, in fact, have the goal of bringing unity to the personality and consciousness from the psychological perspective.

Today we live in a time of spiritual searching. Many people are trying to find new life in their traditional religious institutions. Others are seeking in alternative places such as meditation, yoga, Buddhism, Eastern ashrams, or fellowship houses. But I believe that we all share a deep need to connect with something we may call God, spirituality, or the Divine. Throughout the book I will use the term *Divine* to symbolize the transcendent, spiritual aspect of life. Yet, the influences of Judaism and Christianity, both good and bad, still permeate our understanding of this concept. I think we need to study it anew, as I will do in the book, in order to figure out how our perceptions of these religions and their message may need to transform even if we no longer participate in their institutions.

* * *

The collapse of my religious beliefs early in my life, after my mother died of cancer, injured my ability to figure out what life was all about. It left me more concerned with success than with well-being. My personal loss made me acutely aware, in later years, of a more general absence of the sacred markers that can guide spirituality into becoming a way of life, a way of being rather than a code of behavior. As our religious institutions have rigidified and lost touch with the meaning of spiritual growth, they have also lost their personal relevance for many of us. In the opening section of this book, "The Power of Desire," I explore how this loss has led us to seek concrete, rational answers to our most important questions or to lose sight of the questions altogether in the rush of our complex lives.

Such questions usually throw us into internal conflict because they force us to confront the choice between following our hearts and following a direction defined by our responsibilities to others; that is, what our families and culture consider a "good" or "responsible" life. For over thirty years I've struggled through marriage, divorce, career change and spiritual loneliness, looking for peace and happiness that always seemed just beyond my grasp. Slowly, I learned that psychological and spiritual growth go hand in hand and depend upon my ability to hold the tensions in the conflicts my efforts to evolve bring up. For example, I realized that going back to school and changing careers, following the desire of my soul (the story I shared in *Sacred Selfishness*), would cause me to face a divorce. My wife felt that I was destroying our lives. I felt that my future, my spiritual existence and my health depended upon making this change. Yet I also valued the institution of marriage. No one in my family had ever divorced and I wanted to spare my children a turbulent childhood.

When I first realized how great the conflict in my desires was, it made me sick and I went to bed for three days. Then I realized that I had to go on, one day at a time, looking for the clarity to support every step as I took it. I learned that I must shoulder the tensions of my dilemmas until I fully understood their personal and spiritual implications. Previously, the absence of meaningful sacred rituals and stories in my life had robbed me of a model for holding and exploring these tensions and giving a holy value to the struggle for inner growth. Nothing in my earlier religious education had taught me that I might be experiencing a "dark night of the soul," part of the mystical path of growth—a crucifixion of my own, or the necessity to sacrifice something of great value, as in the story of Abraham and Isaac.

But in time, that changed. As I climbed out of that darkness, I learned that understanding the most challenging questions, the ones about our purpose, meaning, beauty, divinity and compelling desires, begins with trying to understand ourselves. In the course of my journey, one that continues to this day, as I have grappled with these issues and the quests they throw me into as seeker, voyager and wanderer, I have turned to Carl Jung for help. No other spiritual or psychological teacher has provided a model as helpful in knowing myself as the one Jung provided. The spirit of his work brought earth, air, fire and water into my life.

In part two, "The Depth of Soul," I show how we must explore the past in our efforts to learn more about the forces that have formed us, and how we are realizing our potentials for life. This search has brought me face to face with the contradictions that occur when my best intentions fail to bring me fulfillment, or when I find myself unable to carry them out. I want to emphasize that learning to confront these dilemmas by expanding our questions beyond the safe ones, beyond the early rules of right or wrong, provokes the spiritual energy that lies deep within us to surface. In part two, I will also clarify the importance of metaphors in linking us to the source of our creative energy as they can help us understand ourselves and our spiritual teachings.

Learning to know ourselves isn't just a task that has personal benefits. In part three, "Transforming Lead into Gold," I will discuss how society's healthy growth depends upon our growth in self-knowledge. In this respect, learning about our shadow—the aspects of our potentials, along with their desires, that we have denied and repressed in order to fit into the expectations of our families and society—becomes important. Uncovering these unlived parts of ourselves introduces us to the latent fears and promises of delight inherent in personal transformations.

Next, I will explore how our shadow is reflected in our culture, how society goes through cycles of decline, and how we can help it renew itself and become transformed. How we do this actually determines how painful this process will be for ourselves and our neighbors. It is much less painful in the long run to learn how to understand and appreciate people in our society who are different from us than it is to disenfranchise them until they rise up and break through the doors of social acceptance, respect and equal opportunity. Even if we end up opposed to some of their standpoints, we may do so from a place of empathy and understanding.

The path of individuation, our attempt to become more self-aware and to transform our personal lives into their fullest expression, lifts us out of herd mentality and helps us become the makers of our age. The more we grow the more we affect the world around us, avoid a "sickness of the soul," and live up to our responsibilities to each other and future generations.

Wholeness becomes the home for our most vital energies in part four, "The Wedding of Spirituality and Sexuality." In this section our journey, the double flame of our passion—spirituality and sexuality—takes us inward into the realities of our lives. Then it travels beyond ourselves, not into abstractions and idealizations, but into beauty, hope and love, for it is the burning of this flame that expands the boundaries of our fixed ideas about how life should be. While the first three parts of the book help us understand ourselves and our society, as well as the parts sexuality and spirituality play in our lives, this final section shows us how life can become grounded in purpose, cosmic relatedness and love.

As our consciousness grows we gain the powerful realization of how, through the development of our selves, we can create a vessel where life's greatest energies are brought together in a way that stretches love from the beginning of our lives until their end. In making this effort to know the truth of our selves, there is nothing more necessary or potentially transforming than seeking to release the love in each of us struggling against great odds to be born.

PART
ONE

The Power of Desire

What is erotic? The acrobatic play of the imagination.
The sea of memories in which we bathe.
The way we caress and worship things with our eyes.
Our willingness to be stirred by the sight of the voluptuous.
What is erotic is our passion for the liveliness of life.

—Diane Ackerman, A Natural History of Love

Chapter 1

DESIRE'S INITIATIONS

For ever warm and still to be enjoy'd,
For ever panting, and for ever young;
All breathing human passion far above,
That leaves a heart high-sorrowful and cloy'd,
A burning forehead, and a parching tongue.

—JOHN KEATS, "ODE ON A GRECIAN URN"

In the early twilight of a June evening in 1953 I began to burn. I was fifteen years old and embarking on my first date. Overhead the moon was beginning to appear through the fading sunlight. The heat of the day was slipping into the humidity of a Georgia evening. Not knowing whether I was shaking from fear or excitement, I struggled to gain my balance and begin the long trek up the sidewalk to her house. Each step brought a shudder of elation and torment. Finally, I rang the bell. When her father opened the door, I almost collapsed.

A few weeks earlier, the moment when I first saw this young lady at a friend's party had become an awakening that began my journey into the mysteries of life and Eros. Throughout the summer we continued dating. We held hands, went to cookouts and swimming parties. At the drive-in we kissed and wrestled in the back seat of my friend's car.

Looking back, I tend to see this summer as idyllic. But it wasn't. Every moment was charged with intensity, fear, insecurity, bravado and ecstasy. Not the ecstasy of orgasm, but of encountering things that were beyond my previous experiences. As I remember our

3

times together I can't recall having a real conversation about anything. We were too caught in the dance of attraction and lust that descends upon all youth when nature thinks it's time to begin the business of leaving childhood, whether we are ready or not.

As soon as fall arrived and I returned to the boarding school for boys I'd been attending since my mother's death, I discovered that most of my friends had had similar summer experiences. The young lady and I quickly forgot each other. But I haven't forgotten the impact of that summer interlude. After almost five decades, I still find the mysterious force that drove that first moment of eros as provocative as ever.

* * *

From age eight to fifteen I lived with my family in the country. Our home overlooked a beautiful lake surrounded by acres of woods. As a boy I would sit in these woods for hours, watching carefully as life pursued its course around me. Squirrels busily fed, stored food for a later date, and chased each other around in the trees. Ants toiled quietly and intently throughout the day. Birds nested and fed, vibrant little sparks of life that departed and returned with the seasons. When spring arrived, tadpoles emerged in the lake and transformed themselves into frogs before my eyes. And buzzards circled serenely overhead, standing by to clean up nature's hard knocks or the careless waste of human destructiveness.

During these years I learned to look carefully at the world with my own eyes and listen to its many, though often quiet, sounds. Even then I sensed the pattern of another reality pulsing beneath the experiences of my practical life—beneath the roles of school, chores, church, and family. This reality reflected the eternal rhythm of the present passing into the future, into a new season.

Then tragedy struck my family in a way that sent fear and grief tearing through our lives like alternating currents. My happy little sister, just a toddler, was diagnosed with cancer. After surgery and a long hospital stay that stunned us all, she began to recover. But her smiles had been wiped away by the savage healing assault on her body, which left her without a kidney. Shortly after my sister's illness, my mother came down with the same disease. Her diagnosis launched a mystical quest that inspired our friends and community even as their hearts were breaking. I was too young to understand, however, that the only way suffering can find meaning is through personal transformation, and that my mother would be forced to choose between her spiritual quest and desolation.

In those days many people still died at home. Thus, during my mother's illness, our home became a place of activity. Doctors and ministers came by frequently, as did friends and relatives. Eventually, my father was forced to create an early version of hospice by hiring two nurses for around-the-clock care. While we watched my mother's flesh wasting away, many of our friends and extended family members commented on her spiritual transformation. They were deeply moved as she smiled gently through her pain and talked with them, drinking as much as she could from life through her increasing discomfort. Almost everyone who encountered her was touched and spoke in hushed tones of what was happening. One sunny afternoon our minister broke down in tears as he prayed with her and held her hands.

Throughout this time, Eva, our maid, moved quietly through the house humming and occasionally softly singing old hymns of solace and redemption—the hymns that sang of our longing for a better place where we would finally know the peace of being home. Her presence gave the house an ambiance of spirituality that seemed to come from the center of the earth.

My sadness turned to anger at the injustice of my family's pain. And when my mother died, I stayed angry. Day by day as my family sank into despair, I retreated into tearless grief. I found little comfort in religion; my mother's dying had burned through the structure of my life and beliefs, incinerating my image of God as a stern, merciful, loving and forgiving father. Instead, I sought consolation alone in the woods by the lake, where I seemed to find a reality deeper than my everyday life.

Since that time, I have periodically longed for this comforting experience of another reality holding me in its hand. The image of the lake continues to visit me in my dreams. It comes back unexpectedly, but always at those times when my spirit needs bolstering from another realm. It took me several decades to realize that this lake image was a metaphor for the unseen spiritual world, one that could renew my dying spirit and transform my approach to life. I understand well why sages and prophets have always returned to the wilderness for spiritual renewal.

Strangely enough, my early spiritual experiences, unrecognized by me as such, occurred about the time when sexual awakening was ready to churn into my life. How often the dance of the erotic and the spiritual coincide and take us by surprise as they lead us farther in our search for a more profound experience of life.

Transformation and Desire

My early encounters with nature, death, and eros set the stage for how my life would develop. They also provided the context for how I would experience sexuality and spirituality, and how through self-transformation I could bring them together to form a passionate, authentic life. The path of transformation is the course followed by our inborn programming for psychological and spiritual growth. When we consciously try to follow this path we call it our journey into wholeness.

Sexuality crept up on me like a thief in the night, a part of my own nature that caught me vulnerable and unaware. Spirituality, too, came as part of my nature, a need to make sense out of life, to find meaning in my experiences and a purpose capable of inspiring and guiding me. As sexuality pushed me out of childhood, my need to understand the trauma in my life took me into a spiritual crisis, beginning a transformational course that would be at work in me for a long, long time. Transformation was the process hidden from view. It worked like the undertow in the ocean, pulling me toward the depths of the soul, where life gestates. The process of transformation can be symbolized as one of life, death, and renewal or rebirth.

6

The ancients believed that sexual desire represented the creative force of the universe and fueled the process of transformation on many levels. On its most basic level it is the energy that renews the species. In Greek mythology the goddess Aphrodite represented the generative power of sexual energy, the love of sex for its own sake. Her marriage to the god of craftsmanship, Hephaestos, showed that passion and discipline can create art. Her affair with the god of war, Ares, reminds us that the mixture of power and passion can become destructive—which the Greeks illustrated by naming three of their children Terror, Fear, and Excess. Yet, importantly, Aphrodite and Ares also gave birth to the god Eros, who symbolized the potentially transforming aspects of sexuality.

The philosopher Plato argued that when sexual energy is turned from physical satisfaction to the life of the mind, and especially to creative imagination, it leads to a desire for beauty and creation of culture. The mystical and contemplative branches of our Western spiritual tradition believed that if this energy could be turned inward and directed toward the spirit, it would flower into a mystical relationship with the Divine. Yet sexuality never relinquishes its power, no matter how much we think we can refine or redirect it. When the life of the mind, art, culture or spiritual growth forgets the importance of the body as the carrier of this energy, sexuality may return in a darker form as the soul's weapon to transform the situation.

Metaphors and Transformation

When I sought comfort in the woods of my childhood I had unconsciously stumbled into an "archetypal" realm, into the comforting heart of life, and I longed to be held close to this heart. Metaphors like "the comforting heart of life" are the tools we use to help us understand newly encountered aspects of reality by comparing them to a reality we already know. Thus a passion-stricken Romeo proclaims his love by saying, "Juliet is the sun." What he means is that she brings light, warmth, and a feeling of being fully alive into his life. Romeo's metaphor helps us understand how Juliet affects his life.

To illustrate, let me refer to a movie that was popular a few years ago, *Il Postino (The Postman)*. In the film, which is a work of fiction, Mario, the uneducated title character, is sitting by the sea learning about metaphors from a character who is meant to be the real-life South American poet Pablo Neruda. The poet recites a poem about the sea to him.

Mario tells him, "I felt like a boat tossing around on those words."

Neruda replies, "Do you know what you've done, Mario?"

"No."

"You've invented a metaphor."

As Neruda explains how images arise spontaneously, Mario says, "You mean then that . . . the whole world, the sea, the sky, with the rain, the clouds . . . is a metaphor for something else?"

Confounded by this statement, Neruda pauses. Finally, he says that he will answer the question tomorrow. I believe the postman surprised the poet by stumbling into the mystical realm.

* * *

Throughout the centuries mystics have felt that everything we see is a metaphor for a reality beyond our everyday perceptions. In their perspective the objects, events and persons of ordinary existence hint at the nature of the Divine, and indeed make the Divine present in some fashion. In the Eleusinian mysteries of ancient Greece, the predecessor of the Western mystical tradition, visionaries saw the cycle of renewal in nature as a metaphor for how we experience the eternal mysteries of life. We live in the creativity of an ever-renewing world, a world of birth, life, death and rebirth. In this cycle of nature, it is *transformation* brought about by new birth that conquers death.

It is often hard to grasp and accept this simple-sounding reality in a practical way. But once something happens that causes us

to think about ourselves in a larger way and to become dissatis-
fied with our lives, we cannot go back to our old way of living.
We can use all of the practical, hardheaded arguments we can
marshal about how good our life is, how much we've invested in
our current position or how we've no right to complain, but our
little voice of doubt will not be silenced. Even grand plans for a
successful future will only overwhelm it for a short time. We need
to take the step of letting our old personality die so a new and
larger one can be born.

Let me give you several examples drawn from my practice.
Once John became a fairly successful man and began to have a
little leisure time, he started to wonder about his childhood. He
became aware that he was troubled by the fact that his father had
not protected him from his mother's furious tantrums. After careful deliberation he realized that he could no longer continue the
superficial relationship he had developed with his father because
of unanswered questions from their past. He didn't know how his
father would react when he began to question him about this period of their lives. But he felt compelled by his desire to find out
more about the events that had shaped who he was. To proceed, he
thoughtfully and carefully opened a discussion with his father and
waited to see how it would transform their relationship.

Sylvia initially thought her depression was simply "her" problem. Then she slowly figured out that her marriage had gone stale
while her husband was buried in work and responsibilities. Her
depression was the result of her repressed desire for a more loving and vital relationship. With some devoted work, Sylvia learned
that we can't recapture the magic of the past in our relationships.
Simplistic attempts at repair, like a night out, a vacation or redec-
orating the house, don't change much, and the hope of an easy,
comfortable solution usually turns out to have been a disappoint-
ing illusion. Once the magic is lost, something new has to be discovered or constructed. It may mean a new commitment to each
other, a new vision of the future together or new ways of affirming,
understanding and appreciating each other. Once Sylvia and her
husband had become distant from the love they had once experi-

enced, she had to learn how to challenge her relationship in a new way that would help their love and interest be reborn. Of course her husband shared just as much responsibility in recognizing and initiating their needed transformation as she did. But, as in most cases, the person who gains awareness of the problem first needs to go ahead and act.

The same was true of Suzanne, a middle school teacher, who had once loved her job and was now bored by it. She had separated from the joy she had once known in her work. Trying to soothe herself with platitudes about how fortunate she was to have a job in a tight job market, to have such a good boss or to work so close to home, didn't help her for long. Nor did the belief that if she could only finish out her time until retirement, she would finally be free to do what she loved. The compromises she was making to stay in a situation she had outgrown were gradually eroding her soul. In these situations willpower isn't enough. Creativity, risk, struggling and transformation are called for when our soul begins to desire for us to live in a larger way. Suzanne had to find a way to transform her job into something challenging and engaging, and even considered finding a new one.

While I'm talking about our personal experiences, the same principles hold true for our cultural experiences. We cannot return to the days before multiculturalism, or to when more simplistic religious answers sustained us, or when we had a lifelong model for our workplace and personal relationships. We must continue to work for transformation, because it is the vehicle that carries life toward completion.

We do this by fully acknowledging our desires and risking mistakes, not by carefully following the scripts of tradition and expectation, as outlined by our culture and our families. Myths, fairy tales and literature are a reservoir of resources offering vivid and various examples of transformation. Beauty transforms the Beast through the love revealed in the suffering caused by her very human mistakes. Cinderella becomes a princess by risking everything for a joyful evening of living far beyond her seeming potential. The phoenix rises from the ashes after being consumed by fire. Scrooge is transformed by a renewed longing for life after facing his inner demons. These examples of transformation are repeated in story after story, reflecting the wisdom of knowing life's patterns.

It is helpful to remember that we cannot "return to the good old days," nor can we successfully follow a program to produce an "ideal projected future." Nor can even the most "realistic," "hard-headed" work repair a now stagnant and deteriorating situation. For the archetypal pattern of life clearly informs us that survival is achieved only through *transformation*. This is a useful psychological premise that I try to remember whenever I feel like I am trying to swim upstream or find myself in despair over the muddle my life is in.

* * *

If sexual desire represents the creative, transformative force of the universe, then it naturally propels us into the cycle of nature. But what about the life of the spirit, that second powerful aspect of the soul? Is there a cycle of the spirit similar to nature's creative cycle? If there is, are we also compelled into it? And do the two cycles ever intersect? It has taken me years of reflection and struggle to conclude that there is such a cycle, a conclusion I believe my mother also reached as she was dying. The spiritual cycle seeks regeneration by having our life grow barren, frustrating and empty, leaving us stuck between the safety of a flat life that is slowly wearing down our spirit and the desire for a more invigorating way of living.

The longings of our soul for a life of worth, meaning, and purpose may move with less initial urgency than sexuality, but will ultimately build up to the power of a tidal wave. To progress out of a situation that is diminishing our spirit we usually have to let go of many ways we have structured our lives and defined ourselves. In the cases we saw earlier, John may have had to let go of the adage that his father "did the best he could at the time" or that it would be disrespectful to confront him now on such an ancient topic. Sylvia had to risk turbulence and a possible failure in communication in order to try to renew her marriage. Suzanne also had to risk violating conventional wisdom and her parents' teachings about the importance of not threatening her secure status in order to enliven her work. These situations may sound more psychological than spiritual to you. But I believe that whenever we are talking about deepening a relationship, bringing new integrity to it, renewing love or seeking new vitality in life, we are also entering the spiritual realm.

For example, Prince Siddhartha, the future Buddha, discovered that he had to leave a luxurious life and seek to understand suffering and discover life's meaning to satisfy his soul's quest. We too must frequently leave the luxury of the fixed patterns we have lived, often those approved of by our families, friends and traditions, in the search for a life that is filled with vitality. The story of Siddhartha's journey into Buddhahood is a metaphor showing how spiritual birth was an initiation into a new life that would reflect his longing for meaning.

Traumatic events may transform our lives in a similar way. Because of her response to her illness, my mother's experience of cancer became what Jungian psychology calls a *transformational* ordeal, or an initiation in the spiritual sense. At first she fought it, denied it and did everything medically possible to cure it. Then she fully accepted it. Acceptance did not mean that she stopped treatment or gave up hope. She realized, rather, that her illness was the focus of her life. She learned that when we fight against the emotional effects of events that engender true suffering, we may find ourselves crushed by depression. Wisely, she chose to develop her own spiritual path, one of giving up the things she was attached to—including the illusion that she had any kind of control over her life or even the ability to maintain her dignity. She must have figured out that her life was being stripped of everything except love, pain and God. By choosing this path she remained animated until the end.

I don't know how she made this choice. Was it because of her religious background? Did she receive a spiritual call of some sort? Did she have an insight that changed her perception, or a dream?

Or was it simply her desire to find a greater sense of peace and refuge from her suffering? By the time I thought of these questions, the people who might have answered them were gone. But I believe that the question she faced, between spiritual growth and despair, is generally in the background of all our lives.

The fact that a murderous disease can become creative and transforming reflects the paradoxical power of life and spirituality in a stunning manner. I am not speaking of any kind of shallow bliss or reconciliation, but an ability through suffering—emotional or physical—to let go of our human attempt to control mortality. In this way, we are exposed to the great coming and going of life, which leads to a feeling of participation in the secret wisdom of the Divine.

At a Loss for Words

With my mother's death my childhood died. It died in silence, because I was too ruined to cry. It was years before I could talk openly about the incinerating darkness of that time. The effects were so complicated and intense that I couldn't figure out how to articulate them. Nor could I put into words the impact of the destruction of my childhood idea of God.

Our language has become inadequate for exploring and expressing our most intense experiences. It has lost many of its nuances in its everyday use, and we often have to stop and think carefully when we talk about profound experiences or risk trivializing them. "Spirituality" has become a popular term, but it's hard to figure out what it means. For a while its meaning seemed to fade into the mists of our unconscious, losing its poetry, its connection to our hearts, leaving us vaguely haunted by feelings of guilt and religious rules and without a way to experience the Divine. As "spirituality" has become a popular word again, it finds us searching in the religions of faraway places, indigenous peoples and the landscapes of twelve-step programs as we try to figure out its meaning and how to reconnect it to our hearts.

"Eros" is a word that we have almost forgotten entirely, except when we use it as an adjective to mean erotic or sexy. "Sexuality" is another word that we've become frustrated with and tired of because it has been used so much. As a young therapist I quickly discovered our inability to employ the language of a lover in discussing our relationships with each other or with life in general. Instead we talk about our "sex lives" or about the mechanics of communication in relationships rather than how to speak of love from the heart. The field of eros, love in all of its forms, once personified by a god, seems to have drifted into the background of our awareness as we have learned to focus on the practical, the hygienic, the mechanical and the sensational aspects of physical stimulation.

I would like to see the meaning of these words restored and expanded, because they are the symbols that shape our perceptions in these important areas of our lives. We will continue this discussion in later chapters, as we look through our memory to the often-forgotten origins of words like spirit, spirituality, erotic, suffering and others, and what they've meant in terms of understanding human experience in the past. As these symbols in our language grow they can become the contextual markers of a life that it is also growing.

The Key to Real Choices

In the practical world I grew up in, sexuality and spirituality were not considered poetically. The logic of aiming for a successful life left little room for passion and visions. Practically from the moment I was born, I was urged to join society's routines that would march me through life. The ancient mythologies and rituals that had once made sexuality and spirituality passionate elements in life's mystery found themselves stored in dusty libraries along with other pieces of our history. Sexuality was less something to be celebrated and *felt* than something to be *practiced* morally and antiseptically. And the same went for spirituality. A religious vision made public in the middle-class world of my childhood would have been regarded as embarrassing and stigmatizing.

"Spirituality" was a word I rarely heard as a child. "Religion" was a more popular term, and religious matters were generally left in the hands of the clergy. Spiritual development or mysticism, which the religious scholar Evelyn Underhill describes as the "development of spiritual consciousness," was unknown in my early life, even though my parents were well educated and we attended church regularly. While today I would claim that my Protestant mother became a mystic through her journey toward death, for myself, this event shattered my religious perspective. Before I could rebuild it I had to carefully redefine my understanding of what the word "religious" means and how it is different from spirituality and the development of spiritual consciousness.

As I entered young adulthood, the cultural changes of the 1960s swept over my generation. This new tide began breaking our sexual taboos, and simultaneously introduced the idea that mystics might have something to offer us after all, as many of our young people followed their rock idols to India, for example, and meditation became popular. But my particular crisis in spirit didn't begin until my early thirties, initiating my journey into self-knowledge and an existence consciously aimed at growth and renewal. In the space of a few months, my life seemed to twist itself into a giant question mark. In spite of my previous success in business I was afraid to stop and afraid to go on. The depression this conflict caused became a call to learn how to understand and love myself. Actually, I'm sure that if you had asked me at the time I would have said, "Of course I love myself." But that was before I had realized we can't genuinely love somebody we don't know.

Honestly knowing ourselves is no simple task. To begin with, it means accepting who we are, including what we don't like about ourselves. However, this kind of acceptance isn't real until we've constructed a good idea of who we can be at our best and at our worst. Getting to know ourselves also brings the startling realization that while we may think we are adults living a unique life, we are really living scripts written jointly by our society, families, churches, traditions and friends. My previous book, *Sacred Selfishness,* shows the pathway out of these impersonal roles. Experience teaches us that building self-knowledge leads to authentic living, self-love and the awareness that something within us—whether we prefer to call it our true self, the Self or the Divine—cares about us and wants to guide our lives toward their highest potentials.

The process of self-discovery builds inner strength, integrity and compassion. It increases our capacity to love, and these characteristics combine to create a person of substance. Paradoxically, the journey into ourselves soon leads us back into life with new energy and sensitivity. Then it takes us a step further into the dynamics that frame our relationships to other people and the Divine aspects of existence.

The most compelling energies in these dynamics are sexual and spiritual desire. As I've mentioned, passion means more than a sexual urge or religious suffering. It also means to be filled with a great desire for another person, an idea, the Divine or a full life. Both sexual and spiritual desire strongly influence the way we view ourselves as well as how we perceive other people—our outer relationships depend upon how well we have learned to understand ourselves. We may have learned to fear our passion, to deaden it or channel it into things that do not add to our lives—or expect our partners or someone else to kindle the flames of our vitality. At the same time, difficulties in our relationships challenge us to learn to know ourselves better. No matter how we look at our growth, whether from a spiritual or psychological perspective, self-awareness is the key to freedom from our past and gives us real choices. Through growing consciousness, sexuality and spirituality can support our efforts to live more passionately and to understand love in all of its forms.

The Importance of Passion

From the beginning of our efforts to live in tribal groups, the power of sexuality has caused spiritual concerns. Realizing how easily our bodily appetites can throw us into aggression, jealousy, despair and madness, spiritual leaders have tried to develop ritual containers for our passions. Tribal elders and shamans taught sacred forms of sexual behavior to young boys and girls as part of their journey into adulthood. As sexuality and spirituality formed an uneasy partnership, we also discovered that sexuality and spirituality shared a common characteristic—passion.

Both sexuality and spirituality can help us experience life more completely, by teaching us to live as a lover of life and as one who finds the sacred in the sensuous. In both, we may suffer passionately and have our hearts broken. The dark night of the soul experienced by St. John of the Cross is an example of spiritual despair in the Western mystical tradition that comes when the Divine seems to have abandoned us. It is a state similar to Romeo's devastation at finding a dead Juliet. Both are equally heartrending events.

Over the last few centuries, our institutional religions have promoted living a bland life that doesn't risk loving, dreaming and suffering—characteristics of passionate living. When our potential for spiritual fervor is ignored and repressed it can turn base and dangerous, and may even be unconsciously acted out sexually. Over the centuries we've seen how it can fuel fear, rigidity and fanaticism.

Sexuality, like spirituality, is an unrelenting force that will either push us to become more conscious or, if denied, make us alienated and destructive in our sexual and relational activities. The more we try to suppress it, the more powerful it will become, fighting our attempts at control with needs and compulsions that can threaten our self-esteem and safety. Or the energy consumed by our efforts to dominate it may leave our personalities dry and barren. And if we try to ignore its value to our soul and use sexual desire for our own ends, for fun and entertainment or to fill our emotional needs, we add to its power to chase the meaning out of our relationships. Years of personal and professional experience have taught me the importance of appreciating sexuality's mysteries and the symbolism contained in our attractions, repulsions, desires and efforts at love. These metaphors are often seeking to heal us, or to open us to new opportunities to outgrow the molds we are stuck in. Like

spirituality, sexuality often seeks to bring us fresh vitality and liber-
ate the new man or woman emerging within us.

The powers of sexual and spiritual desire remind us that tomorrow lurks within us, the latency to be all that we have not been
before. These energies stir the shifting unseen potentials within all
human life. How we choose to understand and respond to them
will determine whether we grow into wisdom or fall into chaos,
and whether they lead us into fear or delight.

Living in Harmonious Opposition

Sexuality and spirituality had evolved into opposite forces in our
culture long before I became an adolescent. In medieval times, our
Western religious heritage pitted the body, and therefore sexuality,
against the spirit. The body had to be mortified and controlled in
order to release the spirit, and many people still seem to believe this
outdated point of view. I was taught that these two energies were
enemies, as if the Divine hadn't fashioned them both. Yet the aim
of these forces seems to be one of embracing a broader version of
life and the Divine than we had before.

Sigmund Freud recognized that we have an innate urge to resolve
the tensions we find within ourselves. Carl Jung believed, however,
that maturity reflects our ability to hold the tensions in our lives in
a conscious balance. He discussed his position so thoroughly that
the term "tension of opposites" has become well known in depth
psychology. We experience this tension when we are torn between
what we want to do and duty, guilt, shame or a confrontation with
our own idealism.

Many of us have been taught to be so nice or so responsible
that we completely smother any desire to live passionately. I've
known many men and women who would like for their life to be
an adventure, or an expression of what their heart calls out. But
instead they end up in an affair, or with a drinking problem, or depressed, or compulsively anxious and busy, because they are afraid
of hurting relatives or being called selfish or irresponsible. Actually
their courage has failed them when they were called to face the true

tension caused by their contradictory desires. Jung suggests that we diligently explore the forces that pull us in opposite directions, that we strive to understand how they attract us and how they limit us. Holding this tension between desires and responsibilities, and exploring both sides of the issue, usually allows for a creative solution, one we hadn't considered, to emerge as our efforts enlarge our self-awareness.

Holding the tension is also a spiritual exercise. When our lives are stuck or stagnant, we have a spiritual problem, because true spirituality seeks love, vitality, authenticity and the enjoyment of a sensuous existence. We betray our spiritual nature when we seek to resolve our tensions by sublimating them in affairs, addictions, busyness, mindless recreation and other activities.

If we hold the tensions between our desires and the responsibilities and duties defined by conventional wisdom until we grow through them, or beyond them, we will learn how to sustain these forces in a harmonious opposition. When they're held this way their effect on us becomes creative, and this is often soul work at its best.

The yin-yang symbol of the Taoist is a pictorial representation of opposites contained in a circle of relatedness and operating in harmonious opposition. When these forces become separate and isolated they aggressively turn on each other and their output is destructive. Reconsidering the things we think we already understand about sexuality and spirituality as opposites will help us bring them back into a circle of relatedness—the circle of the soul.

It was a long journey into self-awareness that helped me move from seeing sexuality and spirituality as enemies to recognizing them as having an ongoing, often dominant influence in my life. When I sought to understand these dynamics as completely as possible, I discovered that they became the foundation of a passionate life. The challenge to bring spirituality and sexuality into harmony and creativity belongs to every one of us. But we must deal with this challenge in a careful, thoughtful manner, and in a way where we are kind and respectful to each other. Together, we can heal one of our culture's great wounds of the soul.

Chapter 2

SEXUALITY'S PAST

Traditions are the guideposts driven deep into our subconscious minds.
The most powerful ones are those we can't even describe,
aren't even aware of.

—ELLEN GOODMAN, TURNING POINTS

It's always surprising to me how much I can learn from the mythic figures in our literary past. As the goddess of beauty, love and marriage, Aphrodite is one of the most extraordinary of the Greek goddesses and gives us many clues about the place of sexual desire in human life. But there is a duality in her nature, reflected by the double tradition of her birth. In the mythic story we know the best, Aphrodite is born after the original father god, Uranus, is castrated by his son Cronos, and his semen falling upon the sea brings Aphrodite forth. She becomes Celestial Aphrodite, ethereal and sublime, pure and spiritual by nature.

In the other story, we encounter the Common Aphrodite, Aphrodite Pandemos, who is the daughter of Zeus and Desire. This Aphrodite of the people often has harlots in her temples. She is the antithesis of purity and represents physical attraction and sexuality. I find it fascinating that the Greeks contained what we would consider a split between the sacred and the profane in their religious structure.

As the Judaic-Christian influence grew, our culture took the position that sexuality speaks for the instinctual, animal or lower person within us, while spirituality speaks for the higher person, the Divine. But this approach has left us with a worn-out ethical system that pits itself against sexuality and fails to recognize the true place of spirituality in our makeup. We no longer accept the idea of an inherent conflict between morality and sexuality. Our real challenge today involves giving our disowned instinctual selves and passion a proper place in our lives.

Spirituality and sexuality force us to re-examine our idols of practicality and happiness, and to discover that our so-called rational reality is a thin crust covering the truth and meaning of our experiences. To deal with life's complexity, we must look through the outer details and seek their inner message. By taking the time to write down our dreams and use them to reflect upon our outer lives, we can make significant discoveries about how we are living. But the process is difficult because it asks us to find within our battered hearts and hurried lives the passion and courage to let go of our illusions of control and empowerment and to look within, searching into ourselves, our emotions and experiences.

Understanding the Past

On the opening page of *Look Homeward, Angel,* Thomas Wolfe reminds us of the importance of our history as he writes:

> Each of us is all the sums he has not counted: subtract us into nakedness and night again, and you shall see begin in Crete four thousand years ago the love that ended yesterday in Texas.
>
> The seed of our destruction will blossom in the desert, the alexin of our cure grows by a mountain rock, and our lives are haunted by a Georgia slattern, because a London cutpurse went unhung. Each moment is the fruit of forty thousand years. The minute-winning days, like flies, buzz home to death, and every moment is a window on all time.

The history and lore of primitive societies contained the sacred traditions and symbols that supported those societies' spiritual principles. Experiences with nature, including human nature, that inspired either awe or dread were usually symbolized in terms of what today we might call "sacred." Thunder and storms indicated the presence of a powerful god. The fertility of nature was necessary to life and personified as gods or goddesses so powerful that they often required human sacrifices. The sun, vital to existence, was also symbolized by various gods. The journey of human life itself was outlined as a ritual path.

Sacred symbolism helped contain the numinosity of these awe-inspiring experiences and allowed people to attribute meaning to them. Another experience that has been symbolically related to many diverse phenomena throughout the centuries—from the fertility of the earth to the creation of the cosmos—is that of human sexuality.

Many of us may remember that some of the most emotionally charged memories of our lives cluster around sexuality. The first date, the first kiss, the first sexual experience, marriage, and the birth of a child—these moments have numinous qualities. So does the darker side of sexuality—being caught playing doctor by critical parents, being shamed for childhood exploring, sexual abuse, rape, or infidelity. This darker side can wound our souls, casting a gloominess on our personalities that may last for years.

I remember a moment in my early adolescence that I consider both numinous and sacred. It came when my parents decided to speak with me about love and sex. They talked with me separately and neither one of them sugarcoated their words with technical terms or religious clichés. My father spoke about how difficult it was to be a young man driven almost crazy by hormones, desperate for release and feeling the danger of having one's best intentions overwhelmed. As he talked I sat staring at him dumbly, finally realizing that he knew how I felt. He quietly shared that he loved my mother and believed that having a family was the most fulfilling way of life for him, but that it might not be for everyone. He cautioned me by explaining that intensity wasn't the same as love, and that a moment of forgetfulness could thrust a young man into a situation of lifelong responsibility and painful choices long before he was prepared.

My mother, who had by this time already had her first bout with cancer, also talked about love. She recalled the story of how she had met my father, their growing attraction to each other and the love that followed. She disclosed how eagerly they had wanted children and added that while she didn't know much about how boys felt, she considered love and sex to be sacred activities.

Their heartfelt advice was seared into my psyche. Their words became guiding principles for my longings as a young man. Without mentioning right or wrong, sin, guilt or religion, they simply shared their values. By doing so they gave me signposts to guide my way and put sexuality into a loving, spiritual context that provided meaning.

As I entered adulthood, however, I resonated so well with the love and sexuality of Celestial Aphrodite that I had rejected the earthier, more sensual version of Aphrodite Pandemos. For example, when I simply wanted sex to be fun, explosive or a release, I was haunted by my parents' words. Later on in my life, when I was finally in a truly loving relationship, I found it difficult to be relaxed and expressive in sexual matters. I had to work to rediscover the values of Aphrodite Pandemos and learn how to enjoy sensuality for its own sake.

Primitives were instructed in how to handle sexual desire by the wise old men and women, the shamans and ritual elders. These special people blended their extensive personal experience of life with certain intuitive insights that produced a wisdom and consciousness beyond ordinary perceptions of the everyday world. They became evolutionary pathfinders who set the standards for their culture. In their hands, the symbols and forms of sexuality were endowed with reverence. Sexuality was recognized as a biological urge that transcended human control, while at the same time it operated *within* humanity . . . binding, protecting and renewing the species. Therefore, sexuality was sacred, both radiant and ominous. As a corollary, both marriage and childbirth were also considered sacred—and their own spiritual forms.

The eruption of sexuality during puberty ends childhood by ushering in a revolution in our personality. It calls for the birth of our adult identity and for emotional separation from our parents.

The ritual forms for this transition in primitive cultures were hallowed, and as we have neglected to continue and update these forms, we have abandoned our children to their biology. And we have abandoned ourselves, for the emergence of sexuality and the concurrent changes in our body usher in an awareness of our initiation into the pilgrimage of life.

Without an acknowledgment of this transition, many of us remain ignorant of the spiritual purpose and power our bodies now hold. Sacred rituals connect us to life and become expressions of our soul. Thus, when we reduce sexuality and reproduction to mere physical functions and thereby rob them of their mythos, we violate something within us that is more profound, precious and sacred than we imagine. We run the risk of creating "soul wounds." For example, a client working with me who had been married and divorced and through several lovers dreamed one night that she was standing before a huge painting of a man and woman making love. The picture was beautiful and had obviously been painted by a great artist. Slowly, she took a butcher knife out of her purse and began to slash the picture.

When she finished speaking, I asked her what she thought of her dream. What had it represented for her? What did this powerful act of destruction mean? She replied with tears in her eyes. "This is what I've done to my own sexuality. People in the dream were crying out in horror. Something in me is crying out, telling me to stop the destruction. I threw out the old shoulds and oughts because they just made me feel guilty. I felt I had the right to express and enjoy myself. But I'm not enjoying myself and I may be ruining something very dear."

When we lose touch with the spirit and mysteries of life, we often replace them with religious or conventional rules—the "shoulds" and "oughts" the client spoke of, rules that offer little in terms of how to relate with the depth of our souls. Once again we forget that life is more profound than our practical busy world acknowledges; we take the easy way out and abandon our responsibility to teach, guide and inform ourselves and our children. This is unfortunate when our society's institutions take this opportunity to slip their points of view into our collective character to fill these gaps. We often don't even realize the influence of messages coming from the media, advertising, schools, temples and churches. When we unconsciously allow sexuality and reproduction to be taken over by social institutions, we abandon not only their spiritual dimension but also what is most essentially human within ourselves.

My parents gave me a foundation for making sexuality sacred in a very personal way. They did this by sharing honestly and clearly their heartfelt thoughts and feelings about the subject. Talking to me in this way is something I would consider a sacred activity, because my parents, who cared about me, took seriously their responsibility to instruct me in how to meet the future, and believed that sexuality was important, had put careful thought and preparation into our discussions. Without a value structure that supports and guides these great forces that live through us, we may find ourselves like a ship at sea without a rudder.

Our overemphasis on science and technology during the last century has led us to secularize sexuality and reproduction, making them more a matter of technique and hygiene than a matter of soul. While of course beneficial in many ways, this approach has also reduced sexuality to recreation and lifestyle. Ironically, we are culturally obsessed with intimacy and relationships. Daily I see people in my office who think they have a right to pursue an active, aggressive sex life but who are simultaneously confused by how lonely and empty they feel. They have engaged in frenetic sexual encounters in a mistaken search for the understanding and value of a true relationship. So just as the growth of rationalism, science and technology has not set us free, neither has the "sexual revolution." Instead, many of us are more confused than ever, and in pain and chaos.

As we watch the decay of the social forms that once carried the sanctity of sexuality, our *individual* task is to restore that sanctity to our own lives. (This is the task the woman awakening from the dream of slashing the picture realized she was facing.) When we do so, we will realize that the sacred is part of the structure of human consciousness.

Both Jungian psychology and the Western mystical development offer us a way to approach this task. But both approaches
require that we reach back into ourselves and our heritage—the
rituals, wisdom and spiritual practices of older cultures—in order
to bring into the present the important concerns of the soul we
have neglected. Understanding our past helps us understand our
nature and becomes a foundation for the future.

Discovering the Questions

Thirty years of professional practice has kept me partnered with
people caught in the struggles of our time. I have often wondered, as Jung did, why erotic conflicts bring more people into
an analyst's office than any other single problem. But, as Jung
concluded, "In spite of all [the] indignant protestations to the
contrary, the fact remains that love, its problems and its conflicts,
is of fundamental importance in human life and, as careful in-
quiry consistently shows, is of far greater significance than the
individual suspects."

Not a day goes by that I don't talk about a sexual problem
with someone. Sexuality is an issue for children and for teenagers,
for the young, middle-aged, and older. It is a problem for the single, the married, the straight and the gay. And their professional,
social or economic group doesn't matter, either. For as long as I
can remember our self-help books and popular magazines have
confronted us with the fact that sex troubles us more than any
other issue. Though I would clarify this to say sex *and love* seem
to continually disturb us.

Right behind these issues is addiction—everything from alcoholism to eating to exercising. If you are familiar with the
twelve-step programs, you know most are based on the view that
a deeper problem of *spiritual emptiness* is at the addiction's heart.
The Nobel Laureate Octavio Paz claims this emptiness comes because we've traded our spirit for money. I would add that we've
replaced meaning with practicality, knowledge with information,

sensuality with repression—and have thereby sacrificed our ability to love.

However, I can't just blame modern life for my everyday struggle to live with honesty and inner integrity, because I think its complexity actually forces us to grow. The conflicts we face mean we must either give up and go along with the culture, or seek to become more conscious and find new spiritual growth to inspire us. Each of us must journey to discover how sexuality, spirituality, passion and love can bring joy, vitality and fresh meaning to our lives.

Seeing life as a journey is a fairly accepted idea today. Yet when people come to see me professionally, they often explain what they see as their problem, then look at me expectantly. Some even ask, "Okay, *now* what do I do?" Generally, they expect an answer rather than an explanation that this is where the journey begins. In our practical and often optimistic approach to life we tend to see problems as if they were puzzles to be untangled or equations in algebra that need to be solved. As a result, we take the attitude that each problem must be clearly defined, attacked, solved and dispatched, so we can go on to something else. Problems that recur are regarded as signs of failure and lead us to ask where we went wrong. Most people begin from this position, perceiving their life in a linear way. As a Jungian analyst, I believe our inclination to look for formulas to fix ourselves, instead of taking a more comprehensive look at our lives, reduces our search for meaning and transformation to a matter of mechanics and techniques.

Jung insisted that we give up our constant wish to figure an issue out and instead focus our full vitality on "knowing it." He suggested that *knowing* a situation means to see through it, to consider it with the mind, and to understand it through the heart. Only in fully knowing our wounds or unlived desires can we figure out how our soul wants us to attend to them. Jung's suggestion is difficult for most of us to accept because we often don't *want* to know our situations, particularly our difficulties, in their entirety. Wounds that call for a healing journey and meeting our true potentials face to face will cause us to confront the congealed state of our lives and our need for transformation. We would often rather escape them without knowing them; we prefer to blame them on someone or something else. In his argument against freedom and spiritual development, Dostoevsky's Grand Inquisitor said, "man prefers peace, and even death, to freedom of choice in the knowledge of good and evil." It is only human to fall into this trap.

In psychology, when things are not known, we call them *unconscious*, and it's very common to prefer to remain unconscious about the reality of our problems. But if we can be braver and seek to know our situations and ourselves better, we quickly discover that when unconscious things become known, they change, and in this process the very foundation of our problems changes. But to get out of a situation without "knowing it" simply invites its return in another, perhaps more drastic form. *Knowing* it means to have a carefully developed, comprehensive perspective on it. It means fully appreciating our emotional responses, knowing the response of our unconscious—the way in which it reveals itself in our dreams and imagination—realizing our psychological part in the situation, and knowing how the situation is nested in the context of human development in general. Such a process leads beyond problem solving to an enlarged and increased capacity for life.

Believe it or not, this reflects the overall Western tradition of approaching life. In the cradle of developing Western thought, the fundamental operating principle of the ancient Greek oracle at Delphi was "Know thyself." In other words, the oracle held that we must know ourselves even before asking the gods for help. In religious terms, we find that Adam, in one of the ancient traditions, actually chose knowledge over immortality. And in Old Testament tradition, the Judaic tradition, each major event in the development of the Hebrew people, as the writer Elie Wiesel reminds us, "was followed by a surge of study, prayer, mystical quest, meditation, or scholarly endeavor." Their search was not detached and objective; it was a passionate response to life.

We can see this pursuit of understanding unfold in the Book of Job, as Job honors the emotional side of his experience by shaving his head and tearing his clothes, and by relating to it all through his counselors as they discuss, probe, analyze, and dialogue about his predicament and how it confounds their conventional viewpoint. Almost the entire book is in fact a series of dialogues wherein the characters seek to know the meaning of Job's position, and also to outline a suitable response to the problems of life for those who hear the account—which means us. Christ goes a step further and describes this dialectic as being at the center of our very being. As he says in Luke 17, "the Kingdom of God is within you." In his book *The Apocryphal New Testament,* the author J. M. Rhodes quotes Jesus as saying, "The Kingdom of heaven is within you, and whosoever knoweth himself shall find it. Know yourselves."

Jung's suggestion that we should stop trying to figure everything out and instead learn to know ourselves, as the ancients of religion have prescribed, is also echoed by the poet Rainer Maria Rilke. In one of his letters to a young poet, he says,

> I would like to beg you, dear Sir, as well as I can, to have patience with everything unresolved in your heart and to try to love the questions themselves as if they were locked rooms or books written in a very foreign language. Don't search for the answers, which could not be given to you now, because you would not be able to live them. And the point is, to live everything. Live the questions now. Perhaps then, someday far in the future, you will gradually, without even noticing it, live your way into the answers.

By loving the questions, and by coming to know them fully, we turn our experiences into the kind of knowledge that further informs how we live. This process enlarges our personality and increases its relationship with our soul. And it gives us a practice that will deepen our understanding of sexuality and spirituality in the larger context of our life.

Chapter 3

THE DESIRE TO TRANSFORM

The liberating encounter with god/dess is always an encounter with
our authentic selves resurrected from underneath the alienated self. It is
not experienced against, but in and through relationships, healing our
broken relationships with our bodies, with other people and with nature.

— ROSEMARY RUETHER, SEXISM AND GOD TALK

By the time I'd finished college I had responded to my family's
traumatic years by wrapping myself in a cloak of normalcy. I
hoped that establishing my own family and being a good husband,
father and provider would redeem my past. But all that wasn't
enough to make me feel safe. So I turned my vulnerability into
ambition, and my fears of loss into individualism. Supported by
our society's admiration of success, I began to climb.

My confidence had increased by the time I owned my own business. Yet my life was stuck in the cul-de-sac I described in *Sacred
Selfishness*. Depressed and frustrated, I found myself in therapy,
where, after a period of healing my past, I searched into how I had
come to live the life I was living, a life fueled by fear instead of passion. It certainly wasn't something I had chosen in the way some
of my friends had decided to be doctors or lawyers. As part of this
effort, I began to wonder whether or not I should change careers.
During this time, I received a message while I slept. The dream
opened with the vision of a young, golden-haired boy standing in
the distance on the top of a gentle hill. The sun was rising, the
morning mists were disappearing, and I could see the wildflowers

surrounding him swaying tranquilly in the wind. I watched the boy lift his arm and urgently beckon for me to join him.

As I longed to start toward him, I became aware of my surroundings. I was in an elegant Victorian house, standing deep in a long hallway looking out through an open door. Immediately behind me was a large room paneled in dark wood, reminiscent of a traditional English men's club. Seated throughout the room's deep leather chairs were obviously successful men, smoking cigars and pipes, drinking coffee, reading newspapers and talking confidently and companionably with each other.

I looked again at the boy. He gestured forcefully and I began to move toward him. When I stepped through the doorway I felt a strange force grab my legs as though I was being tackled. The force was pulling me back into the house, and I awakened with my heart pounding from the struggle.

"What do you think it means?" my therapist asked quietly.

"I think it's showing me the power of the struggle I'm having of trying to decide whether to leave my business and my desire to follow an unknown future"—I hesitated—"a future that has sunlight and potential but no guarantee." My voice trailed into silence.

This dream crystallized my conflict—the promise of the future and the comfort of the present. As I thought about it I felt a strange exhilaration flowing through me, filling me with confidence and inspiration. But where had this dream come from? Who had sent it? Who is the hidden teacher inside us who is showing us our situation and nudging us toward a course of action?

The Spirit of Becoming

The best human image of the spirit in the history of Western culture is the breath. Our Greek and Hebrew forefathers thought the wind of the spirit brought forth the fire of creativity, and until it entered a man or a woman, he or she could create nothing at all. Thoughts and actions can keep us busy, but nothing is changed, no new path is discovered, until desire brings a spark of creative fire into us.

When I awakened from my dream with the haunting image of the golden-haired boy beckoning to me, I sensed the presence of such a spark immediately. Something stirred, and I got a slight shiver when I recognized the spiritual desire in this dream—a desire for a life that was more adventuresome, authentic and risky than the one I was living. I feared this boy while longing to hurry toward him. I realized that something new was present, that some kind of psychological birth had taken place.

* * *

In 1995 a new version of the first five books of the Bible was published. In *The Five Books of Moses,* author Everett Fox, director of Judaic Studies at Clark University, draws us into the Bible through the power of the original and poetic meaning of its language. In his version of these books, the author notes that God discloses who he is to Moses not with the cryptic "I am that I am," but with the promissory "I will be-there howsoever I will be-there." Other biblical resources, such as *The Anchor Bible Dictionary*, translate different forms of God's Old Testament presence as "He who causes to be." In reading these two translations, I was profoundly impressed by two things. In the Fox translation, the spirit of God is always present, and in the Anchor dictionary it is eternally creative. This suggests that the Divine is always in a state of becoming.

Everett Fox argues convincingly that the notion of God in this ancient tradition was beyond gender, a creative force, and that the spirit of God was reflected in the spirit of becoming. That tells me that the meaning of the scriptures may also be following the creative pattern exemplified by the spirit of God. The scriptures, too, may be in a state of becoming.

Actually, this idea isn't new at all. The Judaic tradition, which parented the Christian tradition, is firmly grounded on the becoming of scripture. Jews are taught that scripture is to be dialogued with, and they have carried on these dialogues for thousands of years. They have accumulated centuries of wisdom through the

Talmud and Midrash in their commentaries. Rabbis, scholars, and other dedicated religious people intensely study the scriptures, the interpretations, and these commentaries, and, through their weekly D'vrie Torah, bring them into the present for both individuals and their culture. This process continually enriches the spiritual foundation of their lives and informs the manner in which the Jewish people approach their future.

If the spirit of God is creative, always becoming, and the scriptures are also in a state of becoming, then it makes sense that the theology and dogma of these religions should also be becoming. Religious dogma as a statement of principles based on the authority of scripture cannot remain rigid if the meaning of scripture is growing and evolving. Nor can theology, whose purpose is to explain and guide our relationship to the Divine, remain static while our understanding of our relationship to the Divine is growing. It is a challenging task for us to keep our religious institutions grounded in this spirit of vitality.

On the surface, these ideas of "becoming," always growing into more than we are today, may sound good and even comforting. But in terms of our actual behavior, humankind doesn't seem to long for growth, but for safety, structure, tradition, sameness, and containment. Freud called this the longing for Thanatos, the longing to stop becoming, the longing for death—because to stop becoming *is* death, psychologically and spiritually. The ambition and individualism I embraced after college was a limited sense of becoming that would have turned into Thanatos if I hadn't begun to heal my past in order to open my future to more authentic living. I believe I would have worked myself into a heart attack before the age of fifty if I had refused to listen to the call to transformation.

I know through my experience and my work that all life is in a state of becoming. Even death occurs so that new growth can begin. The religious traditions support this perspective, and so does Jungian psychology, as seen in the importance it places on the archetypal patterns of transformation.

The Spirit of Eros

One of the most extraordinary creation stories from our mythic past is from the ancient Greeks. It tells us that Eros, the god of sexual desire, was born at the beginning of time, out of chaos, and brought together the sky god and the earth mother. This tale gives us many clues about the complexity and mythological power of Eros, who presided generatively over all and who exemplified the power that energized the cycle of life, death and renewal. Representing the life force on all levels, he encompassed all the dimensions of love: erotic, sexual, romantic, brotherly, spiritual and so on.

On the instinctual level, sexual desire moves us to continue the species and promises that we will live in the memories of our descendants. On a more profound level, it compels us to fulfill the patterns of our unique personal potentials, not only for physical development, but for spiritual and psychological development as well—to follow the path of transformation and the soul's drive for a more conscious and evolved engagement with life. When life becomes stagnant and imprisoned, it is frequently sexuality that brings us new crises, breaking our boundaries and plunging us anew into the cycle of life.

During his work with me, a man had a frightening dream of snakes crawling out of the television set in his living room. The snake is an old symbolic friend of Eros in myths and stories. Its meanings are often contradictory. It symbolizes health and healing on the caduceus, the badge of the physician. The fact that it sheds its skin makes it a symbol of new life and transformation. In both cases it represents the life force. But when we constrict our life energy with fossilized values and assumptions, the snake becomes associated with repressed energy, particularly sexual energy. And it will often attempt to lead us into a transgression that will provoke a strong enough shock to push us across the boundary of our current development. This dream provided the needed jolt for my client. As we analyzed it together, he realized he had imprisoned himself in an impersonal, technical world and was endangering his psychological health.

Desire, as the general imperative to grow, is what plunges us into relationships—with ourselves as well as with other people and society. Not long ago, a woman came to see me because of the obsessive fantasies she was having about her boss. While they weren't overtly sexual fantasies, they were often sensual and included having various adventures, and they puzzled her because in reality she wasn't particularly tempted to become involved with him. I suggested that she begin to think of these fantasies as if they were dreams. In Jungian dreamwork the characters in our dreams frequently represent unexplored aspects of our personality. We began to examine what this woman's boss might represent in her psyche as a potential she was longing to develop, which led her deeper into transformative self-discovery.

Another woman who came to see me was embarrassed by her continued infatuation with construction workers. After several unsatisfying affairs, she wondered why this obsession continued. As we considered what these men might represent, she realized she was longing to develop a sense of earthy, aggressive strength.

In another situation Stuart, a middle-aged manager, shocked himself when he spontaneously reached out and sensually caressed the buttocks of a female colleague. Fortunately for Stuart, the colleague seemed amused at his genuine embarrassment over this uncharacteristic lapse in persona and accepted his apology. But as Stuart struggled with his transgression, he was forced to see how trapped he had become in the image of a manager, which he maintained twenty-four hours a day. Stuart learned that while this image was important in his work, it was smothering his animation and creativity during his off hours, a situation that would eventually become destructive.

I have known many people, men and women, whose attraction to a new person marked a turning point in their lives. Every infatuation, and the fantasies that accompany it, has a lesson plan that can be unraveled by working with the fantasies in the same way that one works with dreams—in a symbolic way. When we carefully examine the basis of our attraction, the characteristics that we are attracted to, and the condition of our lives, it can become enlightening. We must consider if it's time to change and grow, and if we are selling out the values of our heart for practicality and other people's approval. For full development, we all need each other. Desire and longing represent the inner forces that pressure us to develop qualities of relatedness, which bring life to wholeness and completion. Our inner teacher that uses these forces is the Self.

The Self and Reality

The great scholar of mysticism Evelyn Underhill notes that the mystic is one whose soul longs for the Divine and the experience of Eternal Reality. In her classic book *Mysticism: The Nature and Development of Spiritual Consciousness*, she describes reality from a spiritual perspective as having two levels. This first level is secular reality, spelled with a lowercase *r*—the literal, everyday, practical substance of ordinary life. This reality is one of obligations, schools, jobs, payments, retirement funds, grocery stores, social conventions, labels, and other necessities.

In contrast, she notes that we also experience what she calls Eternal Reality, spelled with an uppercase *R*. This expresses the nature of the Divine and eternity. And in it is the source of spiritual values and truths. Underhill takes the position that the material or secular world (reality) is supported by a vastly deeper and larger process of Divine Order (Reality). In a similar manner, the mythologist Joseph Campbell believed that Reality pours all of life's energy into the world, and that our myths and religious stories represent the process of how this energy comes into our experiences of living.

Underhill wrote that all of us have the capacity, through spiritual development, to become increasingly in touch with Eternal Reality, and have it inform and, in fact, become the foundation of our secular reality. Jung followed a similar line of thinking, which he expressed in psychological terms. In his work, these two levels of life relate to different parts of our being. In his autobiography, *Memories, Dreams, Reflections*, Jung noted that he had a "num-

ber-one personality." By this he meant that a part of him had to develop as he grew up that could deal competently with the everyday,
practical requirements of life. In psychological language we refer to
this part of ourselves as our *ego*. This is our overall sense of "I," of
who we think we are. Our ego interfaces with the everyday world
through what we call our *persona*, our public face. When mature,
our persona has many forms that can, as necessary, fit the different
situations we encounter.

Once these primary developmental tasks have been accomplished, we have the opportunity to discover what Jung called
our "number-two personality." This personality is the part of ourselves that lives in Eternal Reality, or what Jungian psychology
calls the *Self*. Frequently, the Self is also referred to as carrying
the image of the Divine, the transcendent, or the "image of God"
within us. This is not to say that the Self is God, but rather that
the Divine spark is *in* the Self, like a seed of truth that has been
planted and is growing and urging our transformation forward.
Our awareness of this inner aspect dawns gradually until we finally realize that a heretofore unrecognized "something" within
us, greater than we are, has been orchestrating our lives from day
one in service to our souls.

This awareness generally comes as we develop a certain amount
of maturity. At this point, we can look back on our life, as I did on
my dream about the golden-haired boy, and recognize meaningful factors in our experiences that had no conventionally explain-
able source. Unexpected paths may have opened, while the door
to something else closed. We may have met a particular person,
felt compelled to say something, write a specific letter, or visit an
uncommon place, and everything after that event was different.
Something changed. It is as if a hidden directive power, outside
of our control, was working through circumstances—often even
against our desires and intentions—to press us in a certain direction. But gaining this awareness is unsettling to our ego and our
rational desire to control our lives, and it may even cause a crisis in
our emotional development.

However you look at us—body, mind, spirit, conscious and un-conscious—all are parts of the same whole I refer to as psyche or soul. The soul is our source of complexity and vitality. The Self is the active center of our soul, it contains our unique being that is always striving to express itself through the growth of our person-ality. Picture the Self as the hub of a wheel centering our life force, arranging our potentials and fostering their development like the carefully spaced spokes that reach from the hub to the rim. The rim acts like our everyday personalities, supporting our progress and movement through life, yet its support rests on the center, the Self. This force pushes us, in the words of Thomas Wolfe in *You Can't Go Home Again*, "To lose the earth you know, for greater know-ing; to lose the life you have, for greater life; to leave the friends you loved, for greater loving; to find a land more kind than home, more large than earth . . . ."

As we mature psychologically through reflection and explor-ing the interior aspects of our lives, we can gain more knowledge about our Self and how it is trying to influence our development. And as we continue to grow, our relationship with our Self will deepen and we will repeatedly grow beyond the bounds of our identity—who we think we are. Of course, who we think we are is just that—who we have been conditioned by our personal envi-ronment to *think* we are. As these boundaries expand, we become more of who we *really* are.

Jung noted that our number-two personality, that part of us grounded in the Eternal Reality of our soul, must to a certain ex-tent be put aside while we are developing our ego. In other words, we have to develop a strong sense of personal identity and enough competence to live in the world before we have the substance—the foundation—for developing a deep relationship with our Self.

There is, however, a danger inherent in this developmental pro-cess. When we have established a strong ego, we tend to think it is our entire personality, just as I once believed I was a businessman, an entrepreneur, creating my own future. In addition, the stronger our ego becomes, the stronger is its tendency toward self-aggrandizement and toward building an emotional wall around its boundaries. If we allow our ego to continue in this direction, we will frequently end up at midlife or sooner feeling isolated and lonely in spite of the apparent successes in our career, or active social and family lives. In these cases, we are likely to become alienated from our own inner nature as well as from other people.

In normal development, a "midlife crisis" is the psyche's effort to turn our ego inward toward a relationship with our Self. Unfortunately many people misunderstand the nature of this crisis and make the mistake of either acting out the new desires they are flooded with in a shallow, concrete manner or suppressing them, hoping to slip by the entire event. In both cases, these people fail to develop the broad maturity of a personality that is growing to completion.

According to Evelyn Underhill, the mystics walked a similar developmental path. They too sought to develop a strong personality, because they believed the process of approaching the Divine requires great strength. Their symbolic image of such a personality was the Green Lion—the lion symbolizing strength, courage, nobility, and vitality, and green symbolizing a vitality not yet spiritually mature. In one of my favorite passages, Underhill reframes this explanation and expands upon it. She points out that the beginning mystic

> is called green because seen from a transcendent standpoint, he is still unripe, his latent powers undeveloped; and a Lion, because of his strength, fierceness, and virility. Here the common opinion that a pious effeminacy, a diluted and amiable spirituality, is the proper raw material of the mystic life, is emphatically contradicted. It is not by the education of the lamb, but by the hunting and taming of the wild intractable lion, instinct with vitality, full of ardor and courage, exhibiting heroic qualities on the sensual plane, that the Great Work is achieved. The lives of the saints enforce the same law.

The symbolism and language in this passage is bold and vivid. It dramatically reverses the timid "be a good boy or girl" approach to spiritual development that many of us were taught as children. But children of ancient times weren't taught the way my generation was. A wonderful old Irish folk tale, "The Priest's Soul," retold by W. B. Yeats, can return us to an older way of teaching, one that makes the mystic's point in a more human manner.

The story begins by stating that in olden days, when the world's greatest schools and possibilities for learning were in Ireland, a boy was born to common people. As he grew he became famous for his cleverness, and soon he was putting his schoolmasters to shame. His poor parents starved themselves to send him to school and make him a priest. He became a great teacher, and prominent people throughout the world sent their children to study with him. As the priest became famous, he also became arrogant and began to teach that people had no soul.

"Whoever saw a soul?" he would ask. "If you show me one I will believe." He confounded bishops and scholars alike with his arguments.

One night an angel appeared and told him he had only twenty-four hours to live. After lengthy bargaining, the angel consented to spare him if he could find someone who believed in the soul. The next day the man began the quest, but it seemed to be in vain, for he had already convinced everyone that souls don't exist.

As he sat by the road in despair, a little child walked by. "God save you kindly," the child said.

The priest stared up. "Do you believe in God?" he asked.

"I have come from a far country to learn about him," said the child. "Will your honor direct me to the best school they have in these parts?"

"The best school and the best teacher are close by," said the priest, and he named himself.

"Oh, not that man," answered the child, "for I am told he denied God, and Heaven and Hell, and even that man has a soul, because he cannot see it. But I would soon put him down."

The priest looked at him earnestly. "How?" he inquired.

40

"Why," said the child, "I would ask him if he believed he had life, to show me his life."

"But he could not do that, my child," said the priest. "Life cannot be seen; we have it, but it is invisible."

"Then if we have life, though we cannot see it, we may also have a soul, though it is invisible," answered the child. When the priest heard him speak these words, he fell down on his knees before him, weeping for joy.

This story illustrates that one must use one's talents, develop them to their fullest, and experience their strength and even the arrogance that comes from this experience. In other words, we must develop our ego by becoming competent and active in the world. When a turning point is reached, through some encounter with the Divine or, in psychological terms, the Self, a spiritual maturity emerges. This maturity leads us to experience life in terms of "the Self" or "soul" and reminds us that there is a potential for wholeness within each one of us.

Growing toward Wholeness

Jung considered that the Self could be symbolized as a mandala, which comprises significant imagery in most of the world's religions. We can find many beautiful pictures of mandalas in his final book, *Man and His Symbols*. Jung considered these intricate pictures as symbols not just of the Self, but the wholeness it is seeking.

The mandala universally presents a typical, symmetrical arrangement of parts in a circular relationship to its center. Religious people throughout the world and throughout time have meditated on mandalas to bring about a state of spiritual centeredness, psychic balance, and healing. For example, we often find mandalas in the beautiful stained glass windows of churches.

In my city, we've been privileged to have several groups of Buddhist monks visit to create vibrant sand mandalas. Striking in their colorful robes, the monks would begin their work intensely on large tables around which people gathered to watch their progress.

Each monk would have six or seven bowls of colored sand—egg-yolk orange, midnight blue, forest green, and dusky gray among them. A monk would put a bit of this brightly colored sand into a large metal cone with a tiny hole at its end. As he gently tapped the cone, grains would trickle out into intricate patterns. First, he'd create a large circle about four feet in diameter. Within the context of this circle, colorful images and scenes would appear: flying birds, majestic tigers, processions of elephants, elegant palaces, labyrinth-like patterns. Each quarter of the design mirrored the opposite quarter. At the end, they'd quietly take their mandalas and brush them into the river flowing through town.

Their work is a meditation on the process of expressing our desire for wholeness. I imagine each figure representing our growth from nature into spirit, moving from tiger to palaces and to labyrinth designs, yet all held within the circle and mirrored with equal importance. Completion brings a return to the flow of life, signifying that the process—growth—is the important aspect that enriches all life.

Watching these monks work reminded me that fulfilling our lives is a journey. There are no tangible, outward levels or goals that mark our way, or the "right" way. If we simply follow a concrete map defined by someone else, we reduce our journey to a trip devoid of surprises, new opportunities and authenticity. If we seek to know our problems and live into their solutions through growth and self-understanding, we begin to transform. In my life, I have intentionally never put the trauma of my mother's death "behind me." Instead, it has remained in the forefront of my consciousness to work with psychologically and spiritually, much like the oyster works with the grain of sand that is its greatest source of pain until it becomes a pearl.

* * *

In his clinical work, Jung found that by examining people's dreams he could discern a pattern that reflected purposeful guidance taking place in the life of the dreamer. Through dream images and stories, the Self furnishes a series of lessons compensatory to the dreamer's normal attitudes and behaviors. Like carefully placed buoys marking the channel of our unconscious, they guide the dreamer's development along a unique course. More than just a state of psychological equilibrium (which might simply be a recipe for boredom and stagnation), Jung believed these patterns represented a growth toward wholeness.

If we begin a similar process of self-observation, one that includes an understanding of the symbolic content of our dreams and fantasies, as well as our emotional responses to our inner and outer worlds, we can discern this dynamic process of self-realization—which Jungians call our individuation process. When we become aware of this process and cooperate with it, that immense, not-directly-knowable part of our personality—the Self—will guide us to manifest an identity founded upon the Divine spark within us.

For Jung, the archetype of the Self was the foundation of meaning. When we consciously actualize and express its intent, we begin living toward our highest good. However, realizing that a wisdom greater than our ego is working to guide our life may bring not only a feeling of awe, but also one of fear. Our ego has fought hard for identity, control, and inner security, and the process of submitting to another internal authority may be painful. But only when our ego is able to dialogue with the Self can the true life of spirit become expressed in our life.

The lessons from the unconscious take various forms. In some cases, they may serve to deflate an overblown image of ourselves. This happened to an important executive during his analysis, when he dreamed he was shining shoes for a living in Grand Central Station. Or our dreams may present us with a comforting image—such as a mandala—when our ego is feeling battered and bruised by life. Another man I was working with was having a rough time emotionally in his life. Then he came into my office looking calm and serene for the first time in weeks. He proceeded to tell me that he had had a beautiful dream the previous night in which he was sitting in the warm sunlight in the center of a lovely garden made up of concentric circles of blooming flowers. As he looked out over the rows of flowers, he knew everything was going to be okay. His unconscious symbolically "centered" him in the midst of a dream mandala. Because of his growing awareness of his inner life, this centeredness carried into his outer life as well, giving him strength and emotional support.

Dreams may also show us the psychological complexes we are living in; or they may show us old recalcitrant attitudes, or potentials, or the spirit dominating our life that we are failing to see. I remember a woman lawyer who dreamed she was locked in her Mercedes as it was speeding through town, through stoplight after stoplight, with many near crashes. After reflecting on the dream, she concluded that she was trapped in an expensive and "driven" lifestyle that was becoming dangerous to her. Such dreams are invaluable. They appear as warnings that clearly outline the destructive course we may be on, while implicitly urging us toward a new sense of values and meaning.

In another situation, Leah, who had worked her way up the corporate ladder, reached a crisis point in her life. Her entire career had been with a company that had just been bought out and was downsizing. Along with a number of her friends, she found herself out of work and facing an uncertain future for the first time in over twenty years.

For days she had been almost too depressed to make it in to my office or to remember any dreams. Then one day she came in full of animation.

"I can't wait to tell you my dream," she said. "I was traveling in Europe. I seemed to be on some kind of quest. I went from country to country. Finally, I ended up in the south of France. I was sitting in a bakery having a cup of coffee and admiring the different kinds of bread. I asked the waiter who the owner was, and he replied, "Don't you know? You are.""

She beamed at me. "That's exactly what I've always wanted to do, and with my severance pay I can do it."

What a surprise for Leah. Her Self had awakened her to the possibility of fulfilling one of her soul's desires. Once we begin to embrace our life journey, our unconscious responds to our efforts. Our dreams become clearer, and even previous non-dreamers report that they are suddenly remembering dreams. In many cases the dreams are so vivid, memorable, and relevant that their meaning is easily discernible.

To summarize, from a Jungian viewpoint, as we mature psychologically and spiritually, we are moving toward a more integrated sense of mind, body and spirit. In terms of the spiritual perspective of the mandala tradition, this inner wholeness corresponds to the totality of the universe; in religious terms, it reflects the Divine essence.

From the Jungian position, if we follow our natural developmental pattern, our passion will eventually turn us toward finding the real meaning and value of our existence. Jung felt that this turning point was generally at midlife. I don't think it is quite that predictable. All manner of events, particularly those of loss and trauma, can initiate this turn. So can living an inauthentic life, as I experienced myself. If we fully permit this inner transformation to proceed, we will allow our Self to become the guiding force in our personality. We will naturally turn more energy, time, and attention toward issues of soul and spirit.

But while this turning point is a natural and even necessary move, it is also a very painful one, for it is characterized by sacrifice. It requires us to sacrifice our cherished image of who we think we are, our ego. Joseph Campbell defined our ego as "What you think you want, what you will to believe, what you think you can afford, what you decide to love, what you regard yourself as bound to." Coming into a conscious, personal relationship with the Self requires us to give up our delusions of having power over life and our desires, and instead to discover what our souls really want. It also means we must begin to accept our own death.

The Irish folk tale I mentioned a few pages ago makes this very point. When the priest/teacher was faced with his own death, he had to give up his arrogant self-image as a man who knew more than nature. He had to listen to the clear voice of a child. The angel, we will recall, had given the teacher twenty-four hours to live. As the story continues, we learn that the teacher's realization came at the end of the time the angel had granted him. Knowing his mortal life could not be spared, he hoped his new awareness would ensure the safety of the soul. He gave his penknife to the child, imploring him to stab him in the chest until he was dead.

"I will pray," said the child, "to have the courage to do this work."

This bloody work symbolizes the sacrifice and suffering we are called upon to make when we must give up the idea of who we think we are. As the teacher's agony ceased, a beautiful creature with four white wings arose from the man's chest. All of the people who were watching knew it was the man's soul. The story then concludes by telling us that this lovely creature is said to be the first butterfly ever seen in Ireland.

Simply put, the tasks of life, according to Jung, involve first developing a personality of substance and a life of one's own, then seeking the deeper Self and living out the full expression of that Self and the particular talents it confers upon us. This process of *personal* development, or individuation, parallels Underhill's outline of *spiritual* development. Underhill states that the spiritual path requires us to become strong and substantial enough to cleanse ourselves of the willful "I want"—the controlling, inflated aspects of our personality. This cleansing enables us to focus our full attention and desire on our relationship with the Divine.

The similarity of these two points of view show how Jungian psychology and Western religious traditions can join hands to point out that while we must become self-responsible, we must also learn that our lives are not fully our own. Our lives belong to the stream of life, and we all contribute to it and experience it through the collective unconscious. In religious terms, one could say that, from this perspective, our lives also belong to the Divine.

Nature and Instincts

As Christianity became institutionalized, it desacralized nature, which means it demythologized it and taught its members to denigrate their instinctual life. I grew up, for instance, believing that anything instinctual meant lower—opposed not only to spirituality but also to such so-called higher functions as thinking and intuition. Spirituality was certainly considered higher than what were regarded as the baser instincts, like sexuality. This bias of Christianity as I learned it reflects the unconscious power of our forebears' religious interpretations.

These old attitudes, as I noted in chapter 1, are still alive and influential in our lives and will doubtless remain so until we wake up to them and reform them.

Initially I was surprised to discover that both anthropologists and Jungian psychologists considered spirituality to be an instinct. This idea had never occurred to me. In Jungian terms, however, instinctual patterns often correlate with archetypal patterns, the psychological templates for our growth.

Anthropologists believe that it is human nature to aspire to a spiritual life, as it is to wish to satisfy sexual appetites and hunger for food. The primitive drawings of religious concepts in the caves at Lascaux in southern Europe demonstrate this. Similarly, the 28,000–year-old cave paintings by Australian Aborigines show that we were engaged in religious activities long before we could articulate in words what we were doing. In contrast, we only learned to give words to the notion of spirit about a thousand years before the birth of Christ. By then we had millennia of great temples, art, and religious edifices throughout the world expressing our instinct, our desire for spiritual expression.

Sexuality and spirituality may be the most powerful instincts we experience, and also the most troubling. As we further explore how Christianity has set these two instincts against each other, we will learn how it has also repressed our ability to find depth and meaning in the mystery of our existence—an ability we can reclaim.

I. The Power of Desire

Questions for Self-Reflection

Understanding what our soul wants comes from loving the questions in our lives and coming to know them fully. This means giving them time and attention and listening to the responses they stir in us.

I invite you to use the questions in this book to begin your personal process of transformation. Read and ponder them. Take your time and consider the thoughts and feelings they awaken. Feel free to change your mind, add more at a later time, be creative, and risk looking deep within as you discover parts of yourself that may have been closed off. If questions of your own arise, add them to your reflections.

- *What were your first experiences of lust, love, infatuation, and death? How did you feel then about these events; how do you feel now?*

- *How was sexuality regarded in your family while growing up? How did your family talk or act around sexual issues?*

- *Describe your relationship to your sexuality. Is sex fulfilling for you?*

- *Do you ever "use" sex for power, distraction, relaxation, the reassurance of feeling loved, or in other ways?*

- *How do you feel about your body?*

- *What recent or chronic physical issues have you had? What are they telling you?*

- *What sexual issues do you have? What are they telling you?*

- *What sexual fantasies do you have? Consider their symbolism.*

- *Have you been sexually attracted to someone other than your partner? What did that other person represent to you? What in the (real or imagined) affair was missing from your own relationship? From your life?*

Befriending Your Dreams

What kind of dreams did you remember while reading this section? What are the images that caught your attention? Befriending a dream (as James Hillman explained to us in his 1967 book, *Insearch*) means writing it down, letting it simmer in your mind, listening to its story, looking at its images and reflecting on them. It also means allowing yourself to feel the dream's moods, the dramatic energy of its scenes, and the intensity or lightness of its characters and story line. Befriending is a kind, personal way of relating to your dreams. It is a gentle process, summarizing how you pay attention, listen, question and reflect upon them. Growing familiar with your dreams in this way is an honest route toward understanding your inner world.

PART
TWO

The Depths of Soul

Two souls, alas, are housed within my breast,
And each will wrestle for the mastery there.
The one has passion's craving crude for love,
And hugs a world where sweet the senses rage;
The other longs for pastures fair above,
Leaving the murk for lofty heritage.

—GOETHE, FAUST

Chapter 4

RETURNING TO THE SOURCE

The muses are the children of the goddess of memory,
which is not the memory from up there, from the head,
it is the memory from down here, from the heart.
It is the memory of the organic laws of
human existence that sends forth your inspiration.

—JOSEPH CAMPBELL, THE POWER OF MYTH

About five thousand years ago the ambition-driven young king of Sumer found himself facing a dilemma. King Gilgamesh discovered that he had pushed the people in his kingdom too far, and they had cried out to the gods for a release from their oppression. As it turned out Gilgamesh was a man split against himself. His ambition had caused him to override the natural, emotional side of himself, causing it to remain primitive and his soul undeveloped.

The first time I heard this story I felt that it was talking about me as well as Gilgamesh. Hadn't I done the same thing when I sought to escape my wounded early life by becoming obsessed with ambition? And later, when I was working in therapy to discover how to change my life, wasn't I really looking for the answers to these questions: What stirs my heart? What makes me really come alive? What gives meaning to my struggles? Or, in other words, what does my soul want? For many years, my ability to ask and answer these questions had been trampled by the power driving my quest for normalcy and success, which I then believed was the road to happiness.

53

As Gilgamesh's story continues, the gods answered the people's pleas by creating a huge man from the earth, a sort of alter ego of Gilgamesh. This man, Enkidu, represented the features of Gilgamesh that he had failed to develop. In psychological terms, he represented the shadow side of the king. In fact, all of us who have been molded by families and society have created our own version of Enkidu as we learned to repress our crude, more earthly characteristics, like our capacity for burning passions, rage, despair, and other deep feeling states—even for joy and ecstasy. In the story the gods believed that struggling with Enkidu would keep Gilgamesh busy and would allow his people to live more tranquil lives, and in fact Gilgamesh and Enkidu grappled with each other vigorously for a long time. Surprisingly, however, they eventually recognized that they were equally powerful and became friends.

Ancient stories like this are subtle and filled with valuable psychological details. They reflect what Joseph Campbell called the "organic laws of human existence," and what Jung referred to as archetypal patterns. In the Gilgamesh story, we see in symbolic terms the journey that this ambitious man had to take to find a meaningful life. The ancient Sumerians also gave us a similar myth, which told the torturous tale of how the ambitious Queen Inanna had to reconcile with her shadow sister, Ereshkigal, in the underworld. My wife and I explore this myth in detail in our book *Like Gold Through Fire*.

Once Gilgamesh and Enkidu became companions they encountered and overcame many obstacles and challenges, including the threat of being consumed by the love of the goddess Ishtar. Finally, Gilgamesh had to defy the gods in order to insure fertility for his kingdom, though the gods struck Enkidu with a mortal illness in retribution. As he mourned, Gilgamesh began the quest for a plant that would bring Enkidu back to life. Finally he found it beneath the water in a pond. But as he was retrieving the plant, a snake snatched it from his hand.

The story underlines a tragic irony of human existence—that as we develop self-awareness we realize the actuality of our death. It also illustrates that to become split in our characteristics wounds our soul, because we cannot develop all of our attributes at once.

At first Gilgamesh lived in denial of this fact. Then he tried to defy death until, tragically, he was forced to accept it. According to Joseph Campbell the acceptance of our death forces us to seek the value of being alive and whole, and to recognize eternity as a presence in our lives. The story also portrays the snake as a symbol of both death and eternal renewal through transformation. The plant brought eternal renewal to the snake, who yearly sheds its skin as a symbol of transformation.

* * *

The *Iliad* is an ancient poem occurring about thirteen hundred years after the epic of Gilgamesh about the quest for love. In this great epic the goddess of discord threw a golden apple marked "For the Fairest" into the midst of the gods and goddesses. Immediately, the goddesses Hera, Aphrodite, and Athena tried to claim it. The young prince of Troy, Paris, was called upon to judge which of the ladies was the fairest. He decided to divide the apple, but none of these powerful goddesses would settle for such a simple, rational solution. From a psychological perspective, the goddess of discord was forcing a choice as to what would be regarded as life's highest value. Would it be home and hearth, the realm of Hera; love and sexuality, the domain of Aphrodite; or wisdom as represented by Athena? Any choice was sure to result in conflict, and to make no choice was not an option. Paris finally chose Aphrodite, the goddess of love and desire, and the rage of the other goddesses unfolded as one of the greatest stories of love, war, and tragedy in the Western tradition.

These ancient stories reveal that, from the beginning of civilization, spirit and desire have defined the human soul and powered the imagination as nothing else does. From a psychological viewpoint, stories such as Gilgamesh and the *Iliad* are metaphors for the archetypal patterns of human development. By studying such tales we can learn more about our own psychological structure, discovering how these archetypal patterns drive and define our lives and times.

We find another example in the great love poem of the Old Testament, the Song of Songs. This work is an expression of unusual passion, love "that is more powerful than death." It relates how the fire that burns in our loins and hearts is a grace that can energize our journey into wholeness. This and many other venerable stories can help us learn how to change our lives for the better and discover the foundations for living a loving, passionate life.

Words, Memory, and Meaning

As I touched on earlier, the words we use have evolved over centuries, moving through the growing experiences of the people and cultures that make up our history. Therefore, many of them carry the memories and meanings, the soul-work, of our ancestors, and we can trace their meaning backward to their origins. In the Western religious heritage, for example, we find that "In the beginning was the Word," and that Adam and Eve were given the power of naming (in effect, bringing into conscious being) all of life's creatures. The existence of this power illustrates the ability of our words to create meaning and reality.

Some of our words have origins older than Abraham. Such a heritage supporting our language is a blessing that binds the present to the past and individuals to groups. Unfortunately, modern life brings a tendency to use words carelessly, only to convey information rather than meaning, while technology and the Internet have created a new Tower of Babel.

Meaning comes from history, nuance, tone, and context. When we hear the words of people close to us and miss the meaning behind them, we are suffering from this loss of depth in our communication. I remember listening to Mike, a young man who told me about his wife's constant complaining. He explained that he had learned to close her off because he felt so frustrated about not being able to make her happy. I suggested that instead of shutting her out or feeling compelled to fix all of the things she was complaining about, he might try simply listening to her until he could discover the meaning behind her complaints—to understand the true concerns behind her words.

How do any of us know we are important to someone if they withhold their words, especially those that have to do with desire and matters of the soul, words of love, delight and other depths of feeling? Likewise, our hearts become barren and empty when we aren't listened to and understood. Then our words either become fewer or rush out in a torrent of anger and resentment. Life and death are in the power of the tongue, the Book of Proverbs reminds us. As we watch our loved ones bloom or wilt as we speak, we discover this to be true.

Making the Sacred Personal

In his book *From the Kingdom of Memory*, Elie Wiesel reminds us to take words seriously by saying that "some part of every word is sacred" and "all words should lean toward the sacred. . . . If our words sound different [now], that is our fault; we forget that God is listening."

Early in this century, the theologian Rudolf Otto tried to counter the loss of meaning in our words due to the surge of rationalism that began in the eighteenth century and continues to deprive them of their ability to express human experience. He wrote *The Idea of the Holy* in an effort to combat these losses that he felt were sweeping through our religious institutions. "Holy," in its earliest origins as a word, also meant wholeness. Otto portrayed the holy as a power far greater than and lying beyond the human realm. It is, he asserted, a power associated with the Divine, or is Divine itself, or is fulfilling the Divine in human actions. To support this he coined the word *numinous*, basing it on *numen*, the Latin word for a Divine spirit or nature god, thereby indicating the presence of the holy. Thus the feeling we have in the presence of the Divine is numinous. We also feel *tremendum*, another term used by Otto to describe the awareness of a mystery, something wholly other from ourselves. A *tremendum* inspires wonder, awe, or dread.

Through words, Otto has helped give us the basis for defining our own personal spiritual experiences. Describing the numinosity of an encounter implies that it isn't the intensity of the experience that matters as much as its quality. An intensely cathartic conversion experience may release a lot of tension without being numinous at all. In contrast, the numinous experience fills us with an uncanny sense of something beyond the ordinary being present, something bigger than ourselves that infuses us with wonder or dread. The experience may be fascinating or comforting, and we may long to repeat it. Or we may be so frightened that it seems to haunt us.

Therefore, when Moses was confronted by a burning bush that wasn't being consumed, as he heard a voice giving him his life's mission, he was having a numinous experience. Mary had a similar experience when she encountered the angel that announced her pregnancy. Saul had one on the road to Damascus. Buddha had one when he left the protection of his father's house and encountered poverty and death for the first time. In the *Bhagavad Gita*, Prince Arjuna had such an experience in the appearance of the god Krishna.

Indeed, most of the great religions are founded on stories of such personal experience. After each one the religious figure is transformed, thrust into a larger frame of reference, which includes an eternal perspective. Each is reminded of a power greater than the individual that is always present and creating new, surprising meaning and purpose in his or her life.

Discovering our personal experiences of the sacred opens us to a relationship with the Divine that we may have a hard time discovering in our religious institutions. When my mother was dying I found little comfort in the doctrines of my church and the simplistic attitudes that God loved me and Jesus was standing there smiling with outstretched arms. I felt betrayed by these teachings and their failure to bring comfort and understanding.

My spiritual experiences came instead in the arms of nature. The night after my mother died I went into the woods and gazed at the stars over the lake. At that moment I knew that I was part of something bigger, supported by my soul. The stars twinkled and made me feel very small, but not alone. I felt a sense of awe that alleviated some of my fear and despair. The experience centered me and helped me through the ensuing year. Later I learned that in Egyptian mythology the soul becomes a star. In other traditions, stars represent the spirit or the spirit as light coming through the darkness.

Numinous experiences often come in times of trauma, illness and despair. And they often come through dreams, visions and synchronistic events—just as they do in the old religious stories. One man who was seeing me had struggled out of an alcoholic past to become a teacher. Currently he was recovering from a divorce and trying to find a new spiritual perspective that would bring him a feeling of acceptance and nurturance. Then he told me the following dream:

> I dreamed that I am going before a tribunal for judgment. I have a strong feeling that I haven't measured up or satisfactorily completed the central task of my life. I am not frightened, but sad. I slowly realize that the group is not judging me, I am judging myself—my life.
>
> Then a series of three transformations begins, each going to a deeper level. The first seems to involve the church. Many people are in golden ecclesiastical clothing and the liturgy and music are majestic and beautiful. I kneel at the communion rail. I do not receive the host, but hands are laid on me and I feel electrified, altered, changed. I cannot tell if something is being added, removed, or both, or neither. But I feel transformed.
>
> In the next level I am in a large, sandstone structure that resembles an early Egyptian temple. There are carvings, incense, and candlelight. Again, the scene is majestic and beautiful, but different from the church. Once more I am touched and electrified. I cry from the sheer beauty of the experience and I am overwhelmed with gratitude.
>
> The final level seems the most modern of all. As before, I

seem to be involved in some transformative process, assisted by
a host of people. There was no setting. No church. No decor.

He stopped speaking, and we sat in silence for a few moments.
Then he went on. "As my eyes opened, I didn't want to wake up
from the dream. I wanted to return, to stay in those places. When
I got out of bed I felt refreshed. Even my body aches and arthritis
pain were gone."

This dream had the characteristics of being numinous for him.
It brought a sense of awe, wonder, and the feeling of the presence of
something larger than himself operating within his life and within
his psyche. He had a hard time leaving the experience of this dream
that he found so engaging and comforting. And in the dream we
see an example of the Self breaking into his consciousness with an
experience of the soul at a time when he very much needed a deeper
connection to life.

Another woman I was working with grew up in a strict, judg-
mental religious atmosphere. Eventually she discovered she was
gay and found a very rewarding relationship. But disapproval and
criticism by several priests and members of her family made her
feel as if she were bad and unfit to take communion. As her inner
conflict deepened, she had a dream of Jesus sensually embracing
her and holding her warmly. Her roiling emotions immediately
eased—she had seen that her sexuality was acceptable in the eyes
of her God, that love, ecstasy and spirituality were not separate
things, but were intertwined. Her desire for acceptance, for valida-
tion of her worth and existence, had been met through a dream,
sent by the Self, from the depths of her soul.

This numinous experience fulfilled a deep spiritual longing
even though it was outside of traditional religious images. Unfortunately, many of our personal spiritual experiences are outside of
traditional structures, and this causes us to either invalidate them
or keep them private. This sadly leads us to think that the things
we value the most, the sacred experiences that touch us profoundly,
have no home in today's religious world.

The late-nineteenth-century psychologist William James referred to our religious institutions as offering "second hand" religions, where we read and study about someone else's experiences. The psychoanalyst Erich Fromm says that when our religions fail to meet our needs to experience the Divine and thereby find meaning and purpose, we will find substitutes to worship, such as materialism, success and achievement. In fact, when we have lost touch with our personal ability to experience the spiritual aspects of life, we may pursue money, success, sex, entertainment or work with religious intensity.

Of course, many of us are able to find personal meaning in our religious traditions. But for those of us longing for spiritual experiences more in harmony with our nature and deepest needs, Otto, along with Jungian psychology, has opened a door to the direct experience of the wisdom and mystery of our souls. And ultimately, more personal spiritual experiences may help us find renewed meaning in or lead to the transformation of our religious traditions.

* * *

Though their theological definitions are different, we generally think of the words "sacred" and "holy" as being identical. The word "sacred" has roots that reach back through French and into the Latin *sacare*, which means to make sacred, or consecrate. The Chicago theologian Mircea Eliade, in his classic book *The Sacred and the Profane*, used a different form of the word "sacred," which came from another Latin form of the word *sacrum*. (*Sacrum* meant what belonged to the gods or was in their power, or what was consecrated). He contrasted the sacred with the profane (from the Latin *profanus*, which meant not consecrated, something that would not be admitted into the temple with the initiates). Eliade also considered that our encounters with the sacred are what give birth to religion. And he pointed out that the sacred and the profane may also distinguish two levels of reality, even though their border may be hard to determine.

The events in our lives frequently cause us to have to become more aware of these two levels. The author and therapist Les

Rhodes explains in her book, *Into the Dark for Gold,* how Parkinson's disease forced her into living these two realities consciously. She notes that she had to figure out "the practical, day-in-day-out problems and challenges of maintaining my quality of life; and an inner spiritual reality concerned with meaning and soulful questions. Who am I now and who am I becoming? This spiritual reality both permeates and transcends my mundane reality."

Remember Evelyn Underhill's treatment of "reality" to represent the profane world, and Reality to mean the Eternal or sacred world. Our religious task then becomes to make life sacred by opening our secular reality—including our bodies and instincts—to deeper spiritual dimensions.

Discovering Spirit

"Spirituality" is one of those words I took for granted until life began to wake me up. Early on, I thought it was the feeling of awe I experienced when watching the sun rise over the ocean, or when standing in a mountain forest, or the wonder at the birth of my children. But as I grew older I figured out that this wonder mixed with reverence is how we respond when we're directly affected by life's mysteries. While these feelings have spiritual overtones, I believe spirituality is more complicated, and goes a step deeper, as it includes the desire to bring the vital force of such mysteries into our experiences and the purpose of our lives.

As the years passed, I realized that my feelings of awe and wonder had never compelled me to begin a spiritual quest, or a search for meaning. Rather, my searches had been put into motion in those moments when I was suffering, feeling confused or stuck, or experiencing the kind of dread that leaves me feeling like my life is slipping from me like water down a drain. Our consumer-driven culture teaches us that we should always be winners, getting the job, the grade, the prize, the promotion, the ideal partner and the happy life. But the real teacher in life, the real agent that compels us to face our life, to re-imagine ourselves, to transform our consciousness, is suffering, failure, dread, loss and grief.

Every new search seems to leave me contending with the meaning of the word "spirit" all over again. I'm not alone in this struggle. Fellow seekers have been grappling with the meaning of this word since it emerged into written language almost three thousand years ago. Our difficulty originates with our need to use verbal concepts to articulate the great experiences of life, which are primarily nonrational. The literal nature of how we interpret and value "rationality" compounds this difficulty. We are so accustomed to valuing the concrete and the objective nature of things that we have trouble expressing the subjective facts of our experience. For example, we may say we want our lives to "work," when we really mean we want them to be more loving, creative, inspiring or interesting.

In daily life we may use the word "spirit" to describe or arouse our emotions in connection with contests and competitions. For instance, we talk about school spirit before a high school football game. Or we may use it to characterize the mood of a particular era or social group. But to speak of *spirituality* we must go further than these everyday meanings.

In its best sense, the word "spirit" becomes a reservoir of the richest experiences and the deepest reflections of human life, a voice of the soul. In its earliest meanings, it described an animating and creative principle, the breath of life, or the metaphorical wind of fire that aroused and inspired us. When we consciously embrace such a spirit and live under its guidance, we will find ourselves living a "spiritual life."

As I previously mentioned, Erich Fromm believed that our culture has made a religion out of marketing and economics, which channel our desires away from our inborn need for meaning. He even had a word for people whose guiding spirit or god, as mine did in my twenties, has become success, materialism, competition and appearances: he called us idolaters. This shift of allegiance has left many of our religious institutions hollow as they serve only the modern principles that run our society rather than the great spiritual truths of the ages. Robert Moore, a Jungian analyst and professor at the Chicago Theological Seminary, notes that religion today helps people "paint up, clean up, fix up," without addressing deeper human issues—a situation he calls one of the tragedies in modern religious life. Part of this problem comes from the inability of these institutions to bring the age-old truths into the context of our modern culture.

The poet Octavio Paz expands this perspective by warning us that "Eroticism has become a department of advertising and a branch of business." He believes that the use of sexuality as a marketing tool has debased both the human body and the human spirit. As a result, the deterioration of sexuality and spirituality has turned the human imagination from love to power in ways that often leave us trapped and wound our soul.

When trying to emerge from my life as an idolater, I had a dream one night in which a number of beautiful native male and female slaves were being brutally beaten. It didn't take much reflection to figure out how mercilessly I was driving myself. In another situation a physician named David consulted me for analysis. David found himself dreaming night after night that he was participating in golf tournaments. With the help of our discussions he concluded that the whole landscape of his life was based on competition. Ellen, another client, had the common reoccurring dream of showing up for an exam unprepared. In a quiet conversation with me she reflected on her drive for success and the anxiety that fueled it, and on how her achievements failed to satisfy her. Under the pressure of our society's values, competition and anxiety had become David and Ellen's guiding spirits, overriding the desires of their hearts, the longings of their spirits and the needs of their souls.

* * *

For Carl Jung, the spiritual problem of humanity was straightforward: if we want to live with meaning, our life must be governed by a spirit of which we are conscious and that is in accord with our highest ideals. He was quick to note that a life lived to fulfill the superficial values of our ego and society, rather than those of our soul, is inadequate, unsatisfactory, and dull for all concerned.

Of course, Jung's perspective isn't a new one. In fact, it illustrates a lesson that must be learned by every age because we forget it so easily. The development of consciousness, culture, and spirituality is a desire that stretches beyond nature's basic parameters. The fullness of life finally requires a "spirit of life" that is profound, independent, and capable of giving vital expression to our human potentials. It is this spirit of life, growing and evolving, that continually informs us on a personal level as to what is sacred despite what our society may value.

My dream of the beautiful, native people being beaten started me on the pathway to realizing that I was living under a false spirit that was hurting me. If my life was going to grow into its true potential, I had to become conscious of the spirit I was living by, how I had unconsciously chosen it, and how I needed to change or limit it. Without such awareness, it would have continued robbing me of the pleasure of enjoying life on a daily basis.

When we try to repress or deny physical, emotional and sexual needs too severely, they find their way into our lives in potentially destructive ways. Before paying attention to his series of dreams, the physician David had been shocked to discover that he had accidentally over-prescribed a drug and almost killed a patient. His compulsive approach to work was exhausting him, causing him to make mistakes. And my other client, Ellen, had become involved in an office affair that could have cost her the success she had worked so hard to attain if it had become public.

Even an ideal that appears noble or Divinely inspired can become so consuming that it robs us of our lives and spiritual growth. In his famous story "The Grand Inquisitor," Fyodor Dostoevsky showed us how a false spirit can often wear the clothes of religion. In this parable, Dostoevsky pits Christ, as he has returned to earth, against the Church founded in his name. The Inquisitor has imprisoned Christ for a second time in history and is justifying his action by explaining that people feel safe and happy when we don't challenge the status quo with ideas of conscience, freedom of choice and spiritual growth. The story implies that Christ will be martyred once again by the forces of conventional wisdom, who wear the mantle of religious and political authority as they invalidate truly sacred spiritual values.

Life and spirit are interdependent and vital powers. Spirit in its best sense gives meaning to our lives and to the possibility of our greatest development. Life is essential to spirit, for it must be embodied and lived or it has no meaning at all.

From Sacred to Secular and Back

My mother's spiritual approach to death touched my life and still does. The same is true of my experience of solace in nature. I've learned that in spite of the troubles and suffering I experienced, there remained a spiritual force that could lift me into the kind of peace that comes from feeling oneness or communion with life.

Turning my back on institutionalized religion, however, didn't mean I was able to walk away from its indoctrination, which permeated the Southern air I breathed. Fall and redemption, original sin, the necessity of blind belief, good works, the inevitability of guilt and punishment—these injunctions haunted me until midlife, when I underwent Jungian analysis and found in it both liberation and exorcism. I discovered, above all else, that the religion taught to me only gave lip service to love and spiritual growth, while being terrified of passion, and that finding joy and sensuality in life might indeed be the Divine's intention.

As I began to study religion more closely, I quickly learned that it hadn't always been the way I perceived it. In her book, *The Battle for God,* the religious scholar Karen Armstrong points out that in the pre-modern world, religion was balanced by two ways of understanding life and acquiring knowledge—*mythos* and *logos.* She notes that both are essential, complementary ways of learning more about the truth of our experiences.

Whenever I walked into the woods to meditate, I was walking into the arms of mythos. Mythos is concerned with meaning, with feelings and the nature of things that are timeless and eternal. Myths of all types have been concerned with the origins of life, the foundations of culture and religion, the meaning of suffering and the afterlife. Mythos is concerned both with our deeper experience of life and its eternal dimension, rather than with practical matters. Depth psychology has discovered that myths are rooted in the unconscious mind and that if we lose touch with their place in our lives, we have trouble seeing the significance of our existence. A lack of meaning, unexplored and unexplained suffering, plus the random cruelty of life can leave us vulnerable to depression, anxiety, despair and even physical illnesses.

Armstrong describes logos as the rational, practical approach to thinking that helps us function in daily life. Unfortunately, in the brash confidence of the modern age, we've begun to rely too much on this approach. And the astonishing success of scientific rationalism seems to have invalidated the importance of mythos. The church I attended as a child, in its effort to follow the trend of the times, tried to abandon the parts of its history that weren't practical, pragmatic or supported by factual evidence. Like many of our religious institutions, it insisted on interpreting the Bible as a literal guide to behavior rather than as a guide to understanding the meaning of life.

Of course, logos has its place. Our modern interpretation of it in situations of illness and tragedy, for instance, has given us a greater capacity to respond with medical and material help. But without mythos we lose the emotional comfort and supportive context that helps us find meaning in these situations as well as the strength to endure them. After I lost my mother, people's well-meaning efforts to console me with rational arguments and shallow explanations — statements like "Her pain is over" or "Now she is closer to God"— only made me angry or more forlorn. Nor could this approach ever give me any understanding of religion's mysteries—Christ on the cross, Moses talking to a burning bush, Buddha's finding enlightenment, or the ultimate value of a human life.

Mythos, on the other hand, expressed in metaphor and poetic

terms, is the very language of spiritual experience. Myth is also associated with the mystical journey, which Armstrong considers a "descent into the psyche by means of structured disciplines of focus and concentration which has evolved in all cultures as a means of acquiring intuitive insight." The mystics and mystical scholars like Evelyn Underhill would go a step further and say that acquiring this profound knowledge provides the ecstatic experience of feeling related to the Divine.

While religion turned away from mythos and the contemplative practices that accompanied it, people like myself, longing to find passion and meaning in their lives and struggles, began turning to analysts and psychotherapists. My own practice as an analyst has so intensely touched and renewed my spiritual life that I consider it a spiritual endeavor in and of itself. Like the mystical path, it deals with a descent into the psyche, a search for deeper meaning and a love of life.

In Jungian psychology, the goal is to keep a sense of balance by having logos as a partner in our effort to revitalize the place of mythos in our lives. Logos also includes philosophy, which in the older sense of the word included the love of knowledge and wisdom. Many of the mystics in the Middle Ages also became Doctors of the Church. They had a great concern that people desiring spiritual growth should not be misled by teachers who were inferior or interested in their own ends. Thus being grounded in both logos and mythos is an important balance.

Logos and mythos are a pair of opposite paths to the soul that should be kept in harmonious opposition during our quest for wholeness. Mythos without logos can create a dangerous cult or a soul unable to fully participate in life. A person who is not grounded in knowledge and wisdom can easily be misled by a charismatic leader, evocative symbols, or their own needs for belonging. On the other hand, logos without mythos lacks a sense of the sacred because it never touches the heart. Knowledge alone is not enough in our search for meaning and must include the values of the heart as we find our place in the story of humanity.

The Fear of Awakening

In Jungian psychology, we learn to look into our soul and into the inner life of humanity to help us see the profound ways the Divine is working in our lives. We call this activity "a search for consciousness." The Jungian approach views the soul as the arena where deeper forces operate, seeing our dreams, visions and dis-eases as ways that a more profound reality is breaking into our awareness.

This psychological approach is a modern version of a venerable tradition. The ancient mystics viewed our everyday state of consciousness as an illusion, a state of "waking sleep." As we grow in self-knowledge we become aware of ourselves as distinct from those living in this illusion. This is the first step in becoming an individual, an authentic person. But this process of awakening can be frightening. We may wake up to discover we're not as in control of our lives as we like to think. We might find we have an aversion to losing control, although it often fascinates us, or that we've developed a revulsion to people who are too loud, too sentimental, too angry, too drunk or too conventional. Some of us are terrified that we may discover how bad or wild we are—that our desires could easily go out of control and threaten the lives we've worked hard to establish.

Our fear often reminds me of a brief scene in the comedy classic *Arsenic and Old Lace*. One of the characters believes he is Teddy Roosevelt, and one day someone asks his sisters: "Have you ever tried to persuade him that he wasn't Teddy Roosevelt?" Once, they reply, "We thought that, if he would be George Washington, it might be a change for him—but he stayed under his bed for days and just wouldn't be anybody."

Most of us, at one time or another, respond to life's demands to grow by symbolically climbing under the bed and hiding from everything new that might threaten our self-image. Many of us become frightened by our teenagers' challenges and appearances, by our spouses or partners changing careers, going to therapy or back to school. Friends getting divorced or declaring a newly realized sexual preference can destabilize us. Sudden flashes of anger or changes in our own or other people's temperaments, or events that make us question the assumptions we've been living by, can scare us. We want to stay secure by convincing ourselves that the principles we've based our lives on are firm and eternal.

The first reaction to our awakening life may be fear as we are catapulted into an inner conflict with our old values and the habits of the people close to us. For example, Tim, a man who had always been a doer, a fixer for family and friends, realized he had little time he could actually call his own. Tim decided to reclaim some time for himself. His brother soon became angry when Tim began spending less time, though still more than anyone else, helping their elderly parents. His sister accused him of becoming cold and selfish after he referred her to professionals for several projects instead of doing them himself. Even his wife became annoyed when he began to put off repairs around the house. But Tim discovered that by persevering rather than giving in to other people's expectations and needs, he began to feel empowered. He also discovered a realistic idea of the nature of his relationships. As he talked openly about his experiences with his wife, she began to appreciate his strength and could laugh with him about how some people were responding to the new Tim.

I also remember Angela, who had always wanted to finish her college degree. She had dropped out when her children were born and delayed re-enrolling in order to help her husband start his business. Now her children were adolescents and she longed to return to school and then go to work. But she was afraid to ask her busy husband and children to take on some of the housework. Angela also worried about how her children would feel if she wasn't at all of their games, and what her friends would think if she stopped participating in school and team support activities. Nevertheless, she decided to take the chance and go back to school rather than risk a life of feeling disappointed.

Fear of alienation from our friends and families often keeps us stuck and frustrated as new awareness is trying to break into our organized lives. We wonder if we'll threaten the people close to us, if they'll still love us and feel comfortable around us, or if they'll reject us. Yet rebirth into a new life of increased wholeness will remain a deep longing in our hearts until we respond to it. Unfortunately, we no longer have a name for this longing, and so it often gets labeled as a disease or emotional problem. But those awakened to the spiritual nature of life's journey will recognize it as the first step on the road toward an authentic and passionate life.

* * *

In the midst of our struggles, if we find that our religious teachers and institutions aren't leading us inward toward the spirit, we must remember that these institutions reflect our own efforts in figuring out how to relate to the Divine. Through a particular group of revelations, a community—a church, a synagogue, a mosque—is formed that supports our efforts. If such institutions are to continue growing spiritually as our culture grows from generation to generation, then we must be active participants stimulating this growth. At the same time, we must beware of giving our religious institutions too much dominion over us. When their purpose becomes power, control and conformity, we should encourage them to instead become advocates for growth, compassion and transformation—the true heart of all religious traditions.

Creative Suffering

One reason we fear change and upsetting the people close to us is that our society has indoctrinated us into overvaluing security and happiness. Our religions have also lost much of their ability to help us endure, value and find meaning in suffering. We have as much of an aversion to suffering as we do to loss of control. In fact, we often connect the two. Suffering people make us uncomfortable, and we are frequently revolted by personal encounters of this expression. We treat suffering as something to be denied, avoided or cured. And we see a person who is suffering as someone to be pitied, someone who is unfortunate, if not dysfunctional or actually pathological.

THE FIRE AND THE ROSE

In the book I co-authored with my wife, *Like Gold Through Fire: Understanding the Transforming Power of Suffering*, we described four categories of suffering: natural, developmental, neurotic, and transcendent. Natural suffering follows such things as natural disasters, illnesses, the death of a loved one, and other things connected with the cycles of life and death. Developmental suffering is also in a sense natural, but results from the painful experiences we encounter as we shape ourselves to take a place in society. Developmental suffering comes when we begin taking responsibility for ourselves, making choices, and suffering the consequences brought on by our decisions. It is part of becoming an adult that hopefully teaches us to be self-disciplined and competent in the world we have to live in. It often means learning to study, attending classes, managing our money, or choosing jobs and careers—tasks that are necessary to live effectively but that don't come naturally.

Neurotic suffering is something that arises from a conflict between longing for growth and a lack of courage to pursue that growth. When we settle for a way of life or give up true inner value for fear of displeasing others, we are inviting neurotic suffering. If Tim had remained Mr. Fix-It for everyone and if Angela had never ventured out of her role as family caretaker, they could have ended up as self-pitying and secretly resentful. Such people become increasingly unpleasant to be around, as they find it more and more difficult to contain their unhappiness and self-loathing. Eventually neurotic suffering sours our lives.

We need instead to become aware that neurotic suffering represents an unanswered call, one that is urging us to discover how to grow and live in a new way. That call can frighten us, because it often asks us to risk much of what we value—indeed the very core of what makes our lives comfortable. So it is not surprising that neurotic suffering may arise from our hesitation to fully commit our energy to pursuing our heart's desire. And yet, giving in to our fear and repressing our desire to grow and change often leaves us stuck, anxious, angry, and depressed.

Our last category, transcendent suffering, comes from following the impetus of the Divine within us to grow in a way that expresses our unique potentials. Over time we have come to call transcendent suffering *creative suffering* because it represents the growing pains of creating and re-creating ourselves in relationship to our greater Self or the Divine within us. It comes from accepting our desire to grow, to want a life we love and feel complete in, and from facing the fears that are holding us back.

Creative suffering usually begins when we confront ourselves in an effort to live more honestly. In Charles Dickens's popular Christmas story of Ebeneezer Scrooge, the demons he faced in the night were pictures of his own shadow. They represented the unconscious values by which he was living, values that had originated in his lonely childhood and were now guiding him toward an isolated, meaningless future. Creative suffering begins as we seek to face and heal the wounds to our soul, discover our shadow, and expand our vision of life.

In the Middle Ages the rituals and traditions of religions carried people through their experiences of natural suffering and helped give a spiritual meaning to them. In times of famine, poverty, illness, or natural disaster, the priest or rabbi offered rituals of healing and atonement, and explanations from scripture that promised a better life in the future. The mystics, too, gave meaning to creative suffering. They took the stance that to become closer to the Divine, one had to go through a painful self-examination and peel off layers of illusion about life and oneself. This was their way of freeing themselves from society's expectations, healing emotional wounds, dealing with their shadow and becoming spiritually authentic.

Suffering in today's world has lost many of its sacred dimensions. Taking time for the spiritual and psychological practices that nurture and transform us—reflecting, journaling, praying, yoga, dreamwork—is often considered selfish or self-indulgent. This is because we have over-learned the cultural command to be active and always doing. Yet, as we saw with Tim and Angela, taking time to listen to our frustration and discontent can change our lives in ways that are ultimately more satisfying—not only for ourselves, but for those we love.

Chapter 5

THE CONTRADICTIONS OF LIFE

She saw now that the strong impulses which had once wrecked
her happiness were the forces that had enabled her
to rebuild her life out of the ruins.

—ELLEN GLASGOW, BARREN GROUND

The above quotation from Ellen Glasgow reminds us that as the Self guides and energizes our journey of transformation, we will repeatedly experience life as a paradox. As Glasgow points out, the desires that seem to be wrecking our life in the present may be the Self at work, serving our soul and creating the foundation of our future.

I left my business and began to study psychology because I liked the idea of helping people learn more about how to transform themselves and their lives. I soon discovered that this big change in direction, which I had struggled so hard to make, was merely a beginning, the first step on a much longer journey. How well this journey was to continue depended upon how much more I was willing to learn about myself. I also had to accept that while this change put me on a road to being more authentic and fulfilled, it didn't mean I would easily find happiness and contentment. Life is wonderful and life is difficult. That's the contradictory reality of the soul.

Our most challenging task is to not deaden joy, wonder and passion in our efforts to cope with the contradictions that life creates. None of us can escape pain, loss, frustration or loneliness. The belief that we can somehow evade or transcend the human condition is a lie. We would be mistaken to believe we are doing something wrong when we find ourselves battered by the experiences of being alive. This is simply the condition of being human.

As I have said, in addition to being difficult, life is also paradoxical. Sometimes doing what appears to be the wrong thing brings the right result. In these cases, the Self is still directing us toward growth and wholeness. When I sold my business and went back to school, even though I had a young family to support, I violated the conventional wisdom of that era. Many members of my family and some friends considered me selfish and even wondered about my sanity. I appeared to be doing the "wrong" thing, yet knew I was being guided by a deeper source.

When a young man, Gary, came to see me he had discovered that his wife, Robin, was having an affair. Gary was shattered. Over time, however, he began to realize that he had wanted Robin as his wife with no cost to himself. He didn't want to risk letting himself be known. He had stayed quiet, uncommunicative and controlled, while always needing to be bolstered by her admiration. Eventually Robin became attracted to a man who was willing to take risks by being more personally open, revealing more of himself, listening and showing interest in her.

Robin's infidelity caused Gary to open his eyes to his own failure as a partner. Paradoxically, it enabled him to access the emotional side of himself so necessary in relationships. His suffering touched the heart of his wife, who had grown cold toward him. Gary was courageous because he was willing to look into the situation for understanding, without taking the way out of thinking of himself as a victim and simply rejecting the person he loved. As a result of his courage, both he and Robin found their personalities and their humanity enlarged by these experiences.

Another woman I worked with had considered herself both a good wife and a successful schoolteacher, and was just as devastated as Gary when she found out her husband was leaving her for another man. After some serious soul-searching Kathleen began to see how she had covered her thoughts and fears about his coolness, and her intuition that he was not fully present in their relationship,

THE FIRE AND THE ROSE

with years of keeping busy. In this case her husband's transgression was the needle that punctured the illusion of a good life that she, as well as he, had been sacrificing to maintain. Our illusions and our false images of ourselves die hard. Yet, once they are dead, we feel a new sense of freedom and inner stability. Kathleen realized that she no longer had to secretly fear an unacknowledged reality and could now pursue a more honest relationship.

While I've learned a lot from my work with people, I first began to notice how often doing the wrong thing transforms life for the better as I was studying fairy tales, legends and religious stories. Many of our best-known stories are filled with characters who change everything with an act of disobedience or even impulsive rage. It seems as if they are urged on by an inner compulsion to act, to assert themselves, even in the face of punishment and disgrace. In fact, if they didn't break the rules of common sense, good manners or ethical behavior, in many cases there would be no heroic adventure and no story to tell. In the legends of King Arthur, the knight Parsifal failed in his first few attempts to find the Holy Grail because he didn't ask the right question. But he didn't ask the question because he had been taught it was impolite to question one's host.

In the fairy tale "The Frog King," a spoiled princess loses her golden ball when it bounces into a nearby well. A frog who lives in the well offers to retrieve the ball if she will become his friend. The princess happily agrees at the prospect of getting her ball back. But as days go by she becomes disgusted with the frog's persistent companionship. Finally she is so sick of him that she snatches him up and smashes him against the wall. Astonishingly, her selfish, violent act transforms the frog into a prince, and the prince and princess fall in love and marry.

Another well-known story tells us about the country woman who has what seems like the good fortune to marry a rich nobleman named Bluebeard. While she enjoys a life of prestige and wealth, her husband gives her the responsibility of taking care of their mansion, with the exception of one room that she is forbidden to enter. She enters it anyway and discovers the mutilated bodies of Bluebeard's six former wives. Her disobedience almost costs her life when her husband detects her infraction. But it also saves her from the fate of the wives that preceded her. When her brother kills her husband, she inherits his fortune.

In story after story we find forbidden acts and irrational behaviors. There are doors that shouldn't be opened, forests that must not be entered, flowers not to be picked, people and creatures that are hideous, and rewards for people who act in disgraceful ways. These tales are meant to remind us how the Self often works to violate practicality or morality and lead us to a new and better life.

Reclaiming Our Depth

When we consider the nature of the Divine, or any of the archetypal forces that support and direct our existence, such as masculine and feminine, life and death, good and evil, and so on, we must accept that certain aspects of their dimensions are fundamentally mysterious. We can experience those forces. But, if we are honest with ourselves, we will admit that we still don't know the final reality of these essential dynamics. This is particularly true with issues of love and sexuality.

In the 1950s the psychoanalyst Rollo May realized that the problems we see in the therapy room are representative of what is happening in our larger society. I was reminded of this fact when I was counseling Martha and Roger, a couple who came to see me about their daughter's sexual behavior. I explained to them how teenagers are different today than when they were adolescents. The peer pressure—to have sex and use drugs—is stronger, and there is little refuge from it. And there is a wall of silence, separation and deception between teenagers and their parents that is more impenetrable than ever before. Sex clubs that stress oral and anal sex—that leave one technically a virgin—abound. Like many parents, Roger and Martha were amazed to hear the facts about what is going on in the world of adolescents. Incidentally, they came to see me because Martha had come home early one day and discovered their daughter Heather, a well-mannered honors student who had never been in trouble, lying nude on the living room floor having sex with two boys.

I also remember Doug and Janet, who came to see me for couples counseling. During their first visit they had confided that their intimate relations had become boring. It takes courage to face up to such a concern. Yet I noticed week after week that when the subject of sex surfaced, one of them skillfully found another topic to focus on. Another patient I was working with was concerned because she had just concluded the last of a long series of affairs. Doris preferred to turn her attention on men's generalized inability to accept intimacy and make commitments rather than to look more deeply into how she was using her sexuality to cover her own insecurities. The reality is that we are all ashamed of sexual dysfunction and are afraid to explore this sensitive area, where the soul has been wounded so often. Instead we pretend the problems aren't there, aren't real, don't mean much, or will go away if we ignore them.

Even if we marshal the courage to get beyond our denial, we still find ourselves trapped in our cultural training, which teaches us to be rational, efficient, productive and independent. This point of view regards our problems as inconveniences that can be isolated from the rest of our lives or packaged into neat little issues, resolvable in a fifty-minute session or two. In Heather's case, she needed for her parents to teach her that she was using her body in a way that would deaden her soul. But to understand how our actions have the possibility to deaden our souls, we first have to face our own lives honestly enough to discover what nurtures and *enlivens* our soul.

It seems unfortunate that our children's problems have become wake-up calls for us to stop ignoring the emotionally complicated aspects of how we are living our own lives. As we guide our young people into adulthood, we ourselves must find the courage to be open in accepting our own struggles and disappointments. Remember that sexual problems, loneliness, and longings for love are part of everyone's growth.

Often a desert must be crossed between our wounds and our healing. Contemplation and reflection can lead us from our ques-

THE CONTRADICTIONS OF LIFE

tions to their answers, but it is a slow, sacred journey. In my own life, I have felt split against myself like Gilgamesh, and my journey home has seemed as long as that of Odysseus. The slower approach that therapy offered me first seemed like a self-indulgent waste of time. But once I was able to quell my need to keep moving and to solve everything, I found therapy a place to let my soul grow. I discovered as well that creativity flourishes in living with the questions, in experiencing life's paradoxes instead of rushing to resolve them.

Sex and Love

Discussing sexuality means discussing love, which is just as problematic for us as sex. When we are children, the love of our parents provides the psychological foundation upon which our lives and sense of stability and well-being will be based. As we grow beyond childhood, love in its many forms, or the absence of love, is the essential feature of many patterns and turning points of our life. I believe that when we are old and reflecting back on our life, we may find ourselves asking, "Who loves me?" "Whom do I love?" and "What has love meant to me?"

Jung reminds us in his essay, "The Love Problem of a Student," that "love is a force of destiny whose power reaches from heaven to hell." From what I see in the media and observe in my professional experience, I have to reluctantly conclude that love and sexuality seem to be spending more time in hell than heaven. Because of the power of these forces within our culture, however, we can no longer afford to leave them to fate, for we and those for whom we care can easily be injured and often devastated by them.

Jung continued his discussion on love by urging us to appreciate its profound complexity in order to understand its problems. We know, for instance, that love, in its breadth, touches every aspect of our lives. Intellectually, we recognize that love's problems can be ethical, philosophical, practical, social, psychological, religious, physiological, aesthetic, and much more. We may use common terms like puppy love, infatuation, or romantic love; psychological terms like projection or need-driven; or spiritual terms such as eros or agape. But love itself is a deeply personal experience that we are in danger of diluting whenever we try to label it. And our labeling may instead distance us from the experience and its real impact on us.

Like love, sexuality is also an intensely personal experience and therefore leads to intense personal problems. Even if we try to consider sexuality impersonally (whether from a clinical standpoint or a recreational one), at the moment "relationship" enters the picture so does spirituality—and we are instantly in the realm of archetypal and transcendent forces, the dimensions of sex and spirit, our two most profound instincts.

Whenever sexuality and love join together in our lives, the result is stormy emotions, uncontrollable longings, deep despair and ecstasy, secret terrors, and other feelings that can be as painful as they are blissful. No wonder Freudian theory reduced all of our problems to issues of sexuality! However, in spite of the raw power of sexuality, the way we deal with it is what is truly important, as it reflects our spiritual view of ourselves. Psychologically, how we deal with sexuality reflects to what extent we love or hate ourselves, and to what extent we are alienated from our soul—and therefore from all life.

Paradox and Contradictions

We may often find that we have the best intentions but end up doing just the opposite, particularly in regard to love, sexuality and spirituality. Our hearts want this and our instincts want that, while our ego is generally overwhelmed by desire or guilt, or is fighting for practical control of the situation. Often, conventional religious training only stresses the management and/or denial of our instinctual and other desires. This approach simply adds shame to our conflicts and therefore offers little help and support to our struggling ego.

This reality brings to mind the writings of the Trappist monk Thomas Merton. On the opening page of his journal, *The Sign of Jonah*, he writes: "The sign Jesus promised to the generation that did not understand Him was the 'sign of Jonah the prophet'—that is the sign of his own resurrection . . . like Jonah himself I find myself traveling toward my destiny in the belly of a paradox."

I love the story of Jonah. Jonah, the prophet, who doesn't participate in any significant events in the Old Testament, seems to have gotten everything in the biblical tradition backwards. When God gives him his only task as a prophet, to go to Nineveh and warn the inhabitants to repent because they will be destroyed in forty days, Jonah refuses to go. Not only does he refuse, but he catches a ship going in the opposite direction. That this little story, only three pages long in the Jerusalem Bible, is even included in the Old Testament seems paradoxical.

Now what kind of prophet thinks he can run away from God? Of course, God kicks up a big storm at sea. And while everyone is trying to survive, we find Jonah down below in the ship asleep. He is finally awakened and the group concludes that some god must be angry. They cast lots to find out whose god it might be, and the mark falls on Jonah. Jonah decides, in a very unprophet-like manner (as he does a number of times in the story), that he wants to die. So he is tossed overboard to save the ship, at which time God has him swallowed by a whale.

After spending three days in the whale without dying, Jonah begins to panic, implores God's forgiveness and consents to undertake the mission he was given. He is released and finally gets to Nineveh, where he repeats God's message and the people repent. Then God changes his mind and spares the people, making Jonah a failure as a prophet, since his one prophecy was false.

The story continues in this paradoxical way. In fact, I would say that this story isn't so much about changing, repenting, or getting life right. It is simply about paradox. In the storyline, Nineveh is saved against Jonah's will, which means he succeeded against his will. He remained a prophet who couldn't see the future, a man chosen by God who refused God, and a man chosen to save people he didn't want to save. Paradoxically, Jonah, who participated in no great events, became an immortal member of a sacred text. And yet his story shows that when we are open to

81

transformation, fate is never sealed and decisions are never irrevocable. I believe this is Merton's meaning in the "sign of Jonah," and that Merton developed these ideas into the notion that life is a whale of a paradox!

Life is full of paradoxes or contradictions that are frequently painful and appear to be beyond our control. But nothing takes us more directly into the fullness of life than these contradictions, particularly regarding sex, love and spirituality. Our actions and beliefs in these areas often seem to be frighteningly at odds with one another. For example, the sexual revolution encouraged us to value our sexual impulses, expression and freedom. At the same time our religious institutions, especially conservative ones, teach that sexual acts outside of marriage are wrong. People caught in these opposing views may end up in despair, confused about what is "right" for them; they may feel guilty over their sexual activities or cheated if they have avoided them.

Reflecting on Merton's writings about life's being a paradox, the spiritual writer Parker Palmer said,

> More than once have I despaired at the corrosive effect of these contradictions on my "spiritual life." I had thought that living spiritually required a resolution of all contraries and tensions before one could hope, as it were, to earn one's wings. But as I labored to remove contradictions before presenting myself to God, my spiritual life became a continual preliminary attraction, never quite getting to the main event. I thought I was living in the spirit by railing against life's inconsistencies when, in fact, I was becoming more frustrated, more anxious, more withdrawn from those vital places in life where contradiction always lurks.

For me, light and liberation appear in Merton's image of life in the belly of a paradox. Perhaps we can be swallowed up by paradox and still be delivered to the shores of our future—just as Jonah was from the belly of the whale. Perhaps contradictions are not impediments to the spiritual life at all, but an integral part of it.

Through them, we can learn that the power for life comes from the Divine, not from us. Whenever we are in the presence of contradictions, soul is always present.

Contradictions are inherent in the nature of life and are related to the spirit of becoming. When in the midst of a contradiction, we may feel ourselves soaring in spirit one moment and screaming at a loved one the next. Or when we achieve our goals, we may find the satisfaction is not so fulfilling or is short-lived. Or we may feel that our beautiful spiritual goals are evading us and then later notice that calm, unseen blessings have slipped into our lives so quietly that we never noticed them. Regardless of their manifestation, contradictions are never accidental.

Transformation and Becoming

One of the most difficult paradoxes we may face is that of midlife, as the following example illustrates. Fred, a forty-five-year-old contractor, came to see me for his depression. It had begun mildly and had sunk deeper and deeper until he was thinking about suicide. Eventually, he was briefly hospitalized. Following that, Fred had continued on various medications for a few more years, but the depression and his thoughts of suicide refused to abate. The stress on Fred and his wife was agonizing.

Now as Fred sat sobbing during our first visit it became clear that he was as confused as he was depressed. He had dreamed since childhood of building houses and having everything that he had now achieved—two beautiful homes, a family, and a successful business that had expanded from the residential market into shopping malls and office parks. Why then, he wondered, was he depressed? Other people, including Fred's wife, parents, and many of his friends, also wondered what he had to be depressed about. Why, after having accomplished so much, wasn't he happy?

In the course of our discussion, Fred asked if there was something wrong with his dream of becoming a builder. He wanted to know if he had latched onto this dream too quickly. Would some other career have been more fulfilling? I thought his original dream was fine. It had taken him a long way in his life. I told him, instead, that I thought he was asking the wrong question. The real question he had been unable to face was what did he need in his life now to awaken his heart? What was his Self trying to tell him through his depression? It seems like a cruel trick to have worked hard, done well and then have to face a turning point rather than simply enjoy the fruits of our labor. Indeed, Fred had stubbornly rejected this crossroads of self-confrontation.

If we can recognize what's happening at these scary or debilitating points in our lives, we usually discover that they are really calls to further development and reflect desires that we have stifled. In our early years, it's commendable to direct our energy outward toward establishing ourselves in the world and building our identity through action and achievement. Fred had done that very well. Jung's theory is that once we have accomplished this, we have to begin directing some of our energy inward, reclaiming parts of ourselves that were lost in the former stage and developing a deeper, fuller orientation toward life.

Psychological midlife is when we begin to turn inward toward a more mature and spiritual orientation as we sense the ending of our physical life. Fred was called to change the hard-driving habits he had developed during the difficult early years of developing his business. His new quest became one of renewing his pleasure in his relationships and of developing a deeper love for life, for his inner life, and for the spiritual aspects of his work. It also helped him to see that building has a spiritual dimension. Houses, for example, are loaded with symbolism and reflect our personalities. They are the container for our relaxation, our disappointments, and our transitions through time.

Fred needed to renew his dreams on a level that fed his soul in a deeper way. He came to understand that the goal of his analysis was not happiness or adjusting to his situation. It was for him to be able to say, "I have never felt so alive."

Some of us get to psychological midlife at a young age, and some of us never get there. Many of us find that the midlife turning point begins an evolutionary process of going within and then returning to the outer world in a new way, over and over again. I've followed this spiral path as I have evolved from a business career to becoming a psychologist and then a Jungian analyst and now a writer. At times it seems unfair that life's path toward becoming whole never offers us a resting point for very long. It continues to advance. But while the path of growth may feel relentless, it also gives us a life filled with love and surprises.

* * *

Life is as paradoxical collectively as it is individually. We may wonder why our technological achievements, our efforts at curing domestic social concerns, and increasing awareness of global issues haven't made the world better than it is. We have had years of antipoverty programs. Why is the number of poor people growing? We spend enormous amounts on medical care, on education, on United Nations relief funds to feed the hungry and to contain the epidemic of AIDS, yet the world basically seems not to be improving. That just doesn't seem fair. We may even begin to wonder what kind of Being created us to stand in the midst of so many seemingly contrary realities.

Thomas Merton's writings have helped me understand that what's important in the face of life's contradictions is how we respond to them. In fact, it is pivotal to our psychological and spiritual development. The places at which we meet the strongest contradictions are turning points—often unexpected, unwanted moments in our lives where we either evade or go farther into the mysteries of life and Creation. This reminds me of the words of the prophet Isaiah in the Old Testament, when the voice of God spoke through him and said: "I form light and create the dark, I make good fortune and create calamity." What we control is not fate, but our response to it.

Jungian psychology shares this perspective and explicitly acknowledges that life is made up of opposites—day and night, joy and sorrow, birth and death, sickness and health. When someone enters Jungian analysis, a confrontation with these opposites is inevitable, at which time things often begin to change rapidly. When clients fully embrace and explore their questions, their awareness of their lives' contradictions is sharply magnified. The religious examination of conscience once did the same thing; however, the spiritual quest for self-knowledge has fallen out of fashion in conventional religious circles and now seems more available in the analyst's office.

Once the inward journey has been initiated, the door opens for grace to enter into the situation, and we often evolve in a manner that we could neither have planned nor predicted. Merton offers us a clear explanation of this process by contrasting the moral with the mystical:

> The difference between the moral life and the mystical life is discovered in the presence of contradiction. When we move ourselves as men, morally, *humano modo*, we end up by hanging on one horn of the dilemma and hoping for the best. But when we are moved by God, mystically, we seem to solve the dilemma in ease and mystery, by choosing at the same time both horns of the dilemma and no horn at all and always being perfectly right.

Merton uses the term "moved by God." We could also use the psychological term "moved by the Self." Merton says that "the difference between the moral life and the mystical life is discovered in the presence of contradiction." We could say the contradiction, "the tension of opposites," reflects the difference between a conventional life and individuation, which refers to our growth into wholeness through developing self-knowledge.

Fred, our building contractor, had tried a logical approach to solving his problem. First he went through medical treatment. When that didn't work, he and his psychiatrist thought a career change might help, so he began teaching in a nearby technical college. But in his case, both moves were actually attempts to avoid the contradiction he needed to face.

THE CONTRADICTIONS OF LIFE

Suppose when I was in my crisis during my early thirties, my counselor had said, "Let's sit down and add up the pros and cons about whether to stay in your business or leave it." The pros would have won without a doubt. He might also have advised that if I was interested in people I could have taught Sunday school, performed volunteer work, coached children's teams, and so on. While all worthwhile activities, they would have missed the point, which was: what was my Self moving me to do through my growing restless discontent? And how could I recognize which desires were emanating not from my head but from my heart?

Knowing the Questions Further

Mystics and Jungians agree on a basic point: we cannot try to resolve the tension of life by disowning its unpleasant aspects and attempting to live perpetually in a bright, pleasant, protected realm—especially one fenced in by safe questions and endless rules about right and wrong. If we hold the world at a distance we are simply "clinging to one horn," as Merton would say. And we will have lost our life, for we will have cut ourselves off from the places where the Divine and the world interact to form turning points of transformation. Living into the contradictions is knowing the questions in their deepest sense and thereby to live into the answers. The "peace that passes understanding," for example, comes from fully accepting the tumultuous and transformative nature of life as it moves us deeper into wholeness.

And as contradictions, or paradoxes, are "lived into," our perception of them is transformed. Paradoxes only *seem* self-contradictory. But on deeper investigation, they are transformational and are actually true. The physicist Niels Bohr notes that "The opposite of a correct statement is a false statement. But the opposite of a profound truth may well be another profound truth." This reflects the fact that as our personality opens to truths and experiences larger than we could have previously comprehended, the Self creates within us a more profound personality.

* * *

Consider this example of being caught between conventional, practical values and the need for living with inner integrity. A woman, Katlin, with several children discovered that she didn't love her husband. In fact, she wasn't sure she had ever loved him. She had married him for a number of good reasons and might even have thought she loved him at the time. But as she matured, she discovered that what passed for love was actually her need to feel safe, nurtured, affirmed, and other psychological insufficiencies that she had now outgrown.

Realizing, however, that her husband Alan had been a good husband and father, and that he and the children would have been terribly hurt by a decision to separate, she decided not to act on her desire for a different life. She wanted her children to have a stable home and was committed to living out an idealized notion of a happy family.

But this vision was not the reality she was living. Laurens van der Post, a writer and friend of Jung's, in a story evocative of just such a situation observes, "Slowly she is poisoning Albert [Alan in our example] . . . The poison . . . is found in no chemist's book . . . It is a poison brewed from all the words, the delicate, tender, burning trivialities and petty endearments she's never used—but would so constantly have spoken if she'd truly loved him."

Van der Post uses this story to make the point that when we live inauthentically, even for the best of reasons, we poison the atmosphere around us and damage the people close to us. This is the destructive or shadow side of this kind of decision. I and most clinicians would also agree that this situation will injure the children, too.

When children sense an absence of love and the undercurrents of resentment, apathy, or frustration in their parents, they lose the sense of security they need as a foundation for healthy growth. Their souls become wounded. If the situation continues, their faith in life may also be diminished, making it harder for them to venture confidently into an independent adulthood. They will very likely become apathetic, angry, anxious, aggressive, or withdrawn and depressed.

It wouldn't be unusual for the children of Alan and Katlin to hide their anxiety in perfectionism and achievement. We might wonder if one or more of them will become promiscuous in a compulsive desire for love, or turn to drugs and peer groups in search of an alternative family. One of them could cause trouble in school, becoming angry and rebellious in an effort to awaken Alan or Katlin from the charade they are living.

Once Katlin becomes aware of the poisoning aspects of her behavior, her ethical choice will become more complicated. To leave Alan would hurt him and the children. Yet, in betraying herself, she is secretly hurting her family and robbing them of their potential to truly experience life and love. She is then, according to Jung, in a tangled position, a *complexio oppositorium*, or complex of opposites. There is no "right" decision.

What should Katlin do? To begin with, she must resist the temptation of practical, either-or answers and, as Rilke suggests, seek to live into the questions, exploring them psychologically. This process starts when she refuses to deny her need for love and authenticity any longer. It will also help her to recognize the conflict between this need and her feelings of responsibility, affection, and kindness toward her family. Holding the tension she is caught in and seeking self-knowledge is the process that will help her "live into the answers" guided by the Self.

Yes, Katlin's process of living into the questions may cause her and her loved ones to suffer. But in this case Katlin will be experiencing *creative suffering*, an enlargement of her heart, in contrast to causing destructive and neurotic suffering. Creative suffering builds an atmosphere that invites the arrival of new meaning and transformation. While Katlin hasn't yet solved her problem, she now has a creative path to follow that may lead to answers she couldn't predict and promises a more fulfilling life for her, and eventually for her family.

Chapter 6

METAPHORS AS BRIDGES TO THE SOUL

The golden light of metaphor, which is the intelligence of poetry,
was implicit in alchemical study. To change magically one
substance into another more valuable one is the
ancient function of metaphor, as it was of alchemy.

—PATRICIA HAMPL, A ROMANTIC EDUCATION

My depression in my early thirties became a challenge from my soul to fill the empty form of my personhood. My response to it generated the search for the kind of self-knowledge that would give me the ability to follow my best instincts and discover the dreams of what I might become. My restlessness had been driven by an energy developing in the depths of my psyche, like oil forming under the pressure of the earth's surface. It signaled that it was time to shift the foundation of my life away from the dark fear and grief from my childhood.

As I strove to cultivate insight into my life and myself, the *Odyssey* became my book of common prayer, guiding me on a journey that was more sacred than any I had experienced in a religious setting. The flame of longing that drove Odysseus through the haunted waters of the eastern Mediterranean likewise pushed me to reject the sleepy Lotus Isle's temptation of a conventional life. Taking in every passage of this great epic until it was a part of me became my path to liberation.

I had fought a war for entry into adulthood and success. Now I longed to find my home in life, where I could live because I loved it and didn't fear the future as an enemy creeping up in the dark. Every insight gleaned from my reading delivered a small shift in my fate. Though I often couldn't explain this feeling, I vaguely realized I had found something to help me discover the path of my soul.

In one famous episode of the *Odyssey*, Homer presents a metaphor of how we have to steer our way carefully between the dangers of being pulled one way or another. In the tale, Odysseus, the voyager, had to travel between the monster Scylla and the whirlpool Charybdis. Scylla had once been a beautiful young woman whom the temptress Circe had cursed and turned into a six-headed monster. She was known to leap out of caves and devour the crews of ships who sailed too close to her. The second terror, Charybdis, was a whirlpool that sucked any vessel sailing close to it into an abyss of destruction. Odysseus and his men had to simultaneously watch each danger carefully as they steered their way between them. Even then, they lost a few men, showing that even when we survive danger we cannot escape without paying a price.

The story taught me that as I worked with my depression, I had to keep the two sides of the situation I faced clearly in mind as I steered my way through them to live into a new answer. Initially I imagined Scylla as the devouring aspects of my successful life as a businessman, which could become consuming. I envisioned Charybdis as the way I might be swept away if I abandoned the rudder of morality, responsibility, and love for my family. Conventional morality and responsibility generally set up the conflict with our need to live authentically that will spur our growth and transformation. I could not simply abandon these conventional values, because, in part, they were genuine for me. I had to steer steadfastly through the contrasting dangers and with the awareness Odysseus demonstrated.

As time has passed I interpret the journey between Scylla and Charybdis more generally, representing the dangers I can fall into if I become emotionally lazy and choose easy answers in important situations. Practically every major decision I've faced—divorce, raising my children and educating them, remarriage, middle age, new vocations, detaching from toxic family members, deciding where to live and where to commit my energy—involved such a journey. It is a journey inward, carefully guided by the values of my heart as they represent my soul.

The *Odyssey* spoke directly to the heart of my experiences. It helped me wake up and say again and again, "Yes, yes, this explains it. This helps me." This story gave guidance and purpose to my journey and meaning to its struggles. It reminded me that life isn't as simple as we are taught, and things aren't always as they seem. Such stories are metaphors that become bridges connecting our everyday experiences with the deeper world of possibilities held by the Self.

My encounter with the *Odyssey* led me to realize that I hadn't even considered looking to the Bible, the religious book of my childhood, for help or metaphors. I strongly believed it gave hypocritical, simplistic answers, that it was an endless source of feelings of inadequacy and guilt. But this is what happens when a resource is robbed of its mythos. I have since discovered that if we lend a mythic ear to these stories, they may inform us in a new way. Being caught between Scylla and Charybdis is a very similar metaphor to Thomas Merton's feelings of being in the "belly of a paradox," an image he took from the Bible.

Metaphor and Western Religion

Today I feel as comfortable identifying with the feeling of being in the belly of a paradox as I do with Homer's image. Both speak to me about experiences of the soul at work. As I read deeper in Merton's work I became even more intrigued with metaphors and the Bible. Then I discovered another helpful book, *The Bible and Us: A Priest and a Rabbi Read Scripture Together*, which shows how useful biblical metaphors are in grasping the complexities of our experiences.

Authors Father Andrew Greeley and Rabbi Jacob Neusner approach the Bible as a poetic work held together by a tissue of metaphor. In their view, the Bible is neither literal nor merely a symbolic representation of truths or generalizations about human experience. Through metaphor, it is to them a direct experience of Reality as it enters our experience of ordinary life. In psychological terms these aspects of Reality are archetypal patterns that support the processes of life. For example, the "spirit of becoming" continues no matter how old we are or what stage of life we are in. If, as Greeley and Neusner propose, we begin to see our everyday lives as metaphor, we will start to see how the "hidden wholeness" of Reality is moving and supporting our life. We will also see how our Self supports us, as these archetypal patterns are not something we could have planned or even conceived of. We will further see, perhaps to our amazement, that this pattern is part of a larger one.

The word "metaphor" has many ancient roots. It originated with the Greek *meta*, which meant over or across, and *pherin*, which meant to carry or bear. In Latin, it came to mean "carry over from one sense to another." Hence a metaphor can create a relationship between two things that ordinarily don't appear logically or rationally related. We will recall the postman in chapter 1 telling the poet Neruda that listening to him made him feel like a "boat being tossed around on a sea of words." Metaphor is the vehicle that communicates to us the postman's immediate experience of being overwhelmed or in awe of the poet's words.

Metaphors are also helpful because they can express a third point of view to carry us beyond a pair of opposites into a more integrated experience of them. I remember a dream I had while struggling with my decision to sell my business and go back to school. I wanted to pursue a new profession with all my heart. Yet the educational path I was considering was lengthy, and I wouldn't have the money to both finish it and also support my children in the way I wanted. This dilemma placed me in the belly of a paradox. To work meant I couldn't throw myself totally into school, and my education would take years longer; if I didn't work, the quality of life with my children would be stressed.

In the dream I was hanging on a cross. While the dream was not foreboding, dark, or bloody, I was still being crucified. Standing below me to my left was a group of children looking up at me.

THE FIRE AND THE ROSE

To my right was a group of older people also looking up. I realized that the children represented the potentials of my future, and the older people carried the traditional values of the past that I didn't want to abandon completely. I knew I simply had to endure the tension of this transitional period. And even though I wasn't religious at the time, this metaphor carried me forward with a sense of certainty and support. I decided to take the longer route through school in order to support my children in the way I wanted and to enjoy my time with them. This path, rather than the more efficient one, enriched my life and opened me to new values of my soul.

The Kingdom Within

The eternal spiritual truths from most mystical traditions are best expressed in metaphors, as they bring a timeless wisdom into our daily experience. In one of his well-known books, Jungian analyst John Sanford uses a verse from Luke in the New Testament—"the kingdom of God is within you"—as a metaphor. Here "kingdom" denotes an aspect of one's wholeness and compares it with the characteristics of a kingdom—in this case, a sense of unity and centeredness that contains feelings of peace, love, and security. Such a place represents the potential that lives within each of us.

In Jungian psychology, archetypal concepts are generally expressed as metaphors. For instance, if symbolic material in a dream or myth speaks of a lion, the sun, or the hoard of gold guarded by the dragon, it may also be speaking of the spiritual power that energizes and supports our life and health. The dream of a psychologically sophisticated professor who had been in analysis with me for several years illustrates this point. He dreamed that a huge, raging bear was chasing him through his house. He awoke from this dream frightened and troubled. I suggested he write out an imaginary dialogue with the bear. Dialoguing, or "active imagination," is a technique frequently used in Jungian analysis, where we dialogue on paper with parts of ourselves, or the images they represent, and actively listen to the responses to expand our self-understanding.

The professor asked the bear who he or she was and why the bear was so angry at him. The bear answered, "I am your unconscious and I'm mad because you are not paying attention to me." Only then did the professor realize that he had gradually stopped his practice of inner exploration. He was no longer writing down his dreams, keeping his journal, and writing the creative essays he enjoyed so much. What was so lucidly presented in the professor's dream would have been difficult for his literal mind to articulate, because the literal mind is generally unable to compare unlike things and fit their meanings into logical formulas.

As each new generation develops, we must find fresh interpretations of the truths or wisdom appropriate to the time we are living in. Otherwise we will lose our rootedness in the past and find ourselves, individually and collectively, in a state of consciousness full of desire but with no awareness of our soul. This can leave us vulnerable to outside pressures such as media and advertising and ultimately unable to build an identity that expresses who we really are.

* * *

Metaphors can also help us understand life poetically, which can be a tremendous comfort. For example, if we consider death literally, it means the end of our existence and offers existential despair. But if we understand death poetically, as a stage in our journey toward psychological or spiritual completion, we can see that it endows our life with meaning and urgency. Such knowledge can open us to an appreciation of the eternity of each moment.

This line of thinking has nothing to do with shallow notions of predestination or fatalism. It has to do with fulfillment. Can we fulfill the life that the Self would like us to have? Can we fulfill the potential that lies within our soul? The answers depend upon our attitudes and the choices we make.

Remember that Divine figures are mysteries that we can experience, though we cannot fully define or conceptualize them. Indeed, Father Greeley and Rabbi Neusner embrace the spiritual practice of anthropomorphizing the Divine, naming it God and giving God human characteristics. Thus a more personal way of relating to the Divine is always open to us through metaphor. Both the Judaic and Christian traditions have a long history of supporting this practice. But we must nevertheless remember that the Divine is beyond our definitions, beyond anyone's definitions. In fact, I think the word "God" is a metaphor for the undefinable Divine. This understanding is particularly important during our era when we strive for political correctness. For example, if we say "God" is "patriarchal," then what we really mean is that *we* have created an image of the Divine that is patriarchal.

Along these lines Rabbi Neusner notes that "if God is only father there's no end to the horror of justice. . . . If God is only mother, then there is no end to the excess of our self-indulgence." He then asks,

> Have I gone too far? Since, the Torah explicitly says, God made humanity in God's image, male and female, I am not claiming more than the Torah says when I compare one aspect of God's life with us to a mother's love for her children; there always is a second chance. But there is the other aspect, and it is a father's love, which is full of expectations. Mercy and justice wed in God's humanity . . . .

However, when we give the Divine human characteristics, we need to be careful to not project images of our early wounding or of needs not fulfilled by our family or our community. For example, when people insist that God is all-loving and all-affirming or is judging and condemning, we can suspect, along with Freud, that they are projecting onto "God" the results of childhood hurts, of their having received insufficient affirmation. Their task now is to bring these parental wounds into their awareness and to heal them. In addition, many people have difficulty accepting the challenges of change, uncertainty, and mystery that life brings and seek safety in a rigidly defined religion and image of the Divine. They too need to discover a more secure ground within themselves, one that is equally anchored in love and authority.

When we realize and, in a manner of speaking, take back a projection, it increases our view of reality and adds to the wholeness of our personality. Projections are often the Self's way of drawing us toward what we really need to heal or develop in ourselves. If we are too self-critical, we need to learn how to show ourselves mercy and love. If we are too self-indulgent, we need to become firmer with ourselves. If we are afraid to change, we need to learn how to deepen our trust in life. We need to find the "mercy and justice wed in God's humanity." We also need to remember that in these cases we have used the Divine as a symbol, when in reality it is still a mystery.

We also often grow psychologically by projecting parts of ourselves onto other people, things, and images and then "recollecting" them—taking them back as we realize they aren't totally valid characteristics of the other person or object. In most cases, they are a combination of truth and projection. However, the projection part of this combination is generally far greater than we would like to admit. For example, I may see an unemployed wino and feel very strongly that he is lazy, despicable, and has thrown his life away. The strength of my response may actually come from my overdeveloped and driven sense of responsibility, which attacks me for "wasting time" in simple pleasures whenever I consider taking a few minutes off. In such a case, my own psychological "stuff" would keep me from viewing this person with compassion or as someone who needs help. This process of recollection, though often painful, is basic to our self-realization, for it expands our consciousness and our personality. At the same time it allows us to see other persons more realistically and relate to them more authentically.

Projections can also be shattered, and if this happens at an inopportune time, the experience can be devastating. I have already spoken about my mother's death and how my childhood image of the Divine died with her. For me to think that the Divine was simply good or loving no longer made sense. But since that time, I have experienced what I consider something transcendent to be working in my life. Now I choose to associate that experience with "God." This attempt at relating to "God" personally causes me to continually rethink my understanding of the Divine. As a result, my image of "God" is always growing, which aids the growth of my self-awareness.

Once we have recollected the "godlike" images of our father and mother in our search for self-knowledge, we can view the Self or the Divine with a less obstructed attitude. Father Greeley and Rabbi Neusner go a step further and say that our relationship with life depends on our attitude toward the Divine, which in turn will respond passionately. Father Greeley notes that "the medieval theologians and mystics believed that all human relationships were metaphors, that they all told us something about the nature of our relationship with God. God was a father, a mother, a lover, a friend, a knight, a brother, a sister." In other words, the Divine is seeking a relationship with us just as we are seeking such a relationship. This doesn't mean the Divine will give us what we want or will rescue us from life's difficulties. But it will passionately respond to our desire for a relationship with it.

The Jungian attitude toward the Self and the soul is similar to that of the mystics. If we turn toward our inner aspects with energy and receptivity, they will support and enrich our lives. To understand these inner aspects, and the nature of all life, we must search for metaphors to explain them, ones relevant to our own personal experience.

Opening the Channels to Life

Many of the great spiritual texts illustrate the value of metaphors. Years ago, while listening to my wife lecture on the psychological meaning of Abraham and his journey, I realized that this story could also have been a guide for me, perhaps even better than the *Odyssey,* in my search for wholeness at midlife.

Abraham's real story begins when he is an older man. He hears a voice urging him to leave the comfortable status quo of life in his father's land and risk everything for the promise of a new country and a renewed future. I could see a parallel to my restless depression as an urging from within to leave old ways and values. Like Odysseus, Abraham also faced a number of trials and challenges. But, unlike Odysseus, Abraham was seeking a new life and a new home, and not a return to an old one. In this search Abraham built a relationship with God, one that began with hearing an impersonal voice and progressed to where he could argue with God. He developed a personal relationship that didn't rest on faith but on his experience.

One friend of mine used the story of Moses as a guide for helping him journey out of the slavery of alcoholism. After years of drinking and several weeks on a binge, he woke up on his living room floor hearing a voice telling him it was time to choose whether to live or die. This was his "burning bush" and the spiritual experience he needed to begin his quest for sobriety.

In her discussion of the Old Testament Book of Ruth in *A Psychological Interpretation of Ruth*, Nomi Kluger-Nash views the woman Orpah through a similar psychological lens. Orpah refuses to return to her mother-in-law Naomi's native land with her after their husbands have died and the famine in that land has ended. Naomi's daughter-in-law Ruth does make the journey with her. Kluger-Nash suggests that Orpah may personify our doubts, our lack of courage and taste for adventure. In other words, Orpah wants to play it safe. This lovely story shows that while safety is not a bad thing, in situations where we are meant to grow our longing for it may become destructive. Orpah becomes a negative figure in the story, because playing it too safe is its own kind of famine, drying up one's spirit and vigor.

There are many other themes in the Old Testament that can inform us and help each new generation find meaning and direction. The patterns of exile, famine, going in search of new lands, renewing one's relationship with the Divine, returning to a time of plenty, and starting new life abound. Famines are caused by drought. I could certainly have identified with that metaphor during my depression. Just as in Orpah's story, famine or drought can mean that our desires have dried up; or perhaps our childhood was too barren, lacking the nurturance and affirmation we needed to feel safe and at home in life. Or it may mean that stress and anxiety have led us into a desert of emotional rigidity. It can also mean our spirituality has become flat and stale.

In these cases a man may become rigid, depressed, or constantly angry; he may become impotent or promiscuous as he searches for new vitality through someone else. A woman may find her body reflecting this same condition as her menstrual periods begin to become infrequent, or her vagina may lose its moisture, making sexual acts painful. The health of our spiritual and emotional life affects our sexual desire. When seen metaphorically, our symptoms are calling us to transform, to leave old attitudes, beliefs, ways of seeing ourselves, and to travel to a new place that is lush and fertile.

We too will have our version of the journey out of bondage, of the Jonah experience, the temptations in the wilderness, the desire and longing in the Song of Songs, and other pivotal moments outlined in this book. Metaphors that strive to bring the largeness and the meaning of life and spirit into our lives in an immediately understandable fashion help us see *what* is happening to us, *how* it is happening to us, and how what is happening is an expression of life supported by a deeper meaning. Religious stories can guide and comfort us when we are stuck or wounded, and in chaos they can guide us on our way.

In his book *The Power of Myth*, Joseph Campbell summarized Jesus' temptations in the wilderness as the temptations of economics (the good life); of politics (power in the community); and of spirituality (the inflation of being above the ordinary). He also described the three temptations of Buddha as being lust, fear, and the submission to public opinion. If you remember the case of Fred, the depressed building contractor who was experiencing a midlife crisis, you may recognize these as the same forces he was battling.

This comparison helps illustrate how archetypal patterns expressed in stories as metaphors are still alive in our life today.

Adam and Eve Reinterpreted

The story of Adam and Eve gives us another example of archetypal patterns. Of course, I wasn't brought up to look at Adam and Eve psychologically. As a fledgling Presbyterian, I learned that "God" created a perfect world and put Adam and Eve in it. They could have lived happily ever after, too, until the snake tempted Eve, who then tempted Adam to eat the forbidden apple. God, of course, caught them, shamed them, and expelled them into a life of toil and struggle that ended in death.

What my young, impressionable mind gleaned from this story is that we humans did something wrong. If we had been good, life could have been another way—we could have been eternally happy. Reflecting today, I am amazed at how deeply I incorporated this simple message. It left me believing that I'm not good enough, that I don't deserve love, that I am flawed and must earn whatever love I may receive. I even wondered when I was a boy if I had brought on my mother's illness. I thought that whenever I was suffering and struggling, it was because I had done something wrong. Psychologically this perspective is literal, shallow, and basically in error. It is in error because the simplistic ideas of "do right, feel good; do wrong, get punished" do not fit either the complexities of our personalities or the world we live in. And the cause-and-effect model of living, even if you accept it, cannot be so simply reduced. Nevertheless, we have developed a culture around this error, along with the false assumption that living in the real world is a punishment instead of a sacrament.

The story of Adam and Eve, as I interpret it, is a metaphor to inform our experience of life today. And therefore we can interpret it as we would a myth. We can say that Adam, as scholars say his name implies, symbolizes humanity—all of us. Eve, as woman, symbolizes life, as the image of woman generally does in mythology. The snake represents desire, the longing for the continual renewal that causes all of life to be in a state of eternal becoming. The snake also symbolizes the deep instinct within us that seeks, through the apple, a symbol of wholeness, knowledge of life through the heart.

We may even go further and imagine—more now from a psychological viewpoint—that the snake symbolizes the desire that seduces and compels us, often through love and sexuality, into the conflicts of life and the transformations through which we must pass. When any of us, as members of humanity, desire to be fully alive in life, we experience a "fall," or a transformation, that marks our development, a process we will repeat again and again. Simply understanding that this pattern exists and that everyone must deal with it can be helpful and comforting. To discover this knowledge we must realize that metaphor is the vehicle that delivers it.

If spiritual writings like the Bible are going to help us in our growth and development, we must approach them with more than just literal interpretation, so that they can inform our lives. We must return the quality of mythos to them, which makes them personal and relevant. People in the Middle Ages used this metaphorical approach, and as a result, these stories became part of their substance, their path to surviving life, finding meaning, solace and hope.

There are many ways to interpret the story of Adam and Eve, but this one has helped me understand more fully that happiness isn't based on following the rules or "getting it right." Nor does the image of the Divine in this interpretation appear as distant and tempestuous as he did in my Presbyterian heritage. Also I am reminded that both the snake (instinctual energy and desire) and the woman (life itself) are integral parts of the Divine. We can use stories like this to help us recognize our calls to transformation and the role of metaphors as bridges to our soul.

II. The Depths of Soul

Questions for Self-Reflection

• *What early life experiences shaped your relationship to spirituality?*

• *Describe your vision of a fulfilled, authentic life.*

• *What is your definition of spirituality?*

• *Who or what do you worship?*

• *Where does the Divine/God/your higher Self appear in your life?*

• *Describe your most significant personal experience of the sacred.*

• *How have the events in your life formed a pattern? For what might they be a metaphor?*

• *What myths, stories, or sacred texts have personal meaning to you?*

Befriending Your Dreams

What was the nature of the dreams you remembered while reading this part of the book? Were there any religious images, childhood images? Were any of them dreams that have occurred before? If so, consider their plots and symbolism.

PART
THREE

Transforming Lead into Gold

The difference between transformation by accident and transformation
by a system is like the difference between lightning and a lamp.
Both give illumination, but one is dangerous and unreliable, while the
other is relatively safe, directed, available.

—Marilyn Ferguson, The Aquarian Conspiracy

Chapter 7

THE SHADOW

Society decides which of its segments are going to be outside of its borders. Society says, 'These are the legitimate channels to my rewards. They are closed to you forever.' So then the outlawed segments must seek rewards through illegitimate channels.

—KRISTEN HUNTER, THE LANDLORD

In my last two years of high school, I became known to myself and others as someone who was going to achieve a lot in life. Yet, by my second year in college, my ambition and potentials had become as foreign to me as visitors from outer space in a 1950s movie. When I look back, I see a lost young fellow who seemed to have stayed drunk his whole sophomore year until a determined young man began to crawl out of the chaos and pursue success with the devotion of a monk. If I look back at pictures of that young man, I have a hard time recognizing the face staring intensely back at me.

That year I also saturated myself in a sea of reading—Freud, Marx, Bergson, Marcuse, Dostoyevsky, Tolstoy, Koestler. My fascination with existentialism—the French philosophical school of the

1950s that focused on man's isolation and estrangement from him-self—led me to a new group of friends. Like myself, these young people had become disaffected from the boot camp approach to education at Georgia Tech and preferred to drink beer and talk about books and their themes of life and meaning, or the lack of the same. My memories of those times, however alcohol-infused, seem more wonderful than dark, for the seeds of my desire for wholeness began to grow then.

A passage from Leo Tolstoy's *The Death of Ivan Illyich* was forged into my psyche and causes deep stirrings in me still, as its lightning words flash through my undying inner storm. These words urge us beyond barely lived lives and push us to know ourselves:

> It occurred to him that what had appeared perfectly impossible before, namely that he had not spent his life as he should have done, might after all be true. It occurred to him that his scarcely perceptible attempts to struggle against what was considered good by the most highly placed people, those scarcely noticeable impulses which he had immediately suppressed, might have been the real thing, and all the rest false. And his professional duties and the whole arrangement of his life and of his family, and all his social and official interests, might all have been false. He tried to defend all those things to himself and suddenly felt the weakness of what he was defending. There was nothing to defend.

One of those Saturday afternoons when I was sitting in Leb's Delicatessen drinking beer, eating cheese, and talking with my friends, "alienation" became our topic. This discussion led us to Albert Camus's enigmatic 1956 novel *The Stranger*, first published in England as *The Outsider*. No doubt our fascination with this book reflected our own unhappiness with our institution's practical, scientific approach to learning, which simply ignored the question of how to live one's life. In that decade, technology and engineering offered the promise of the future and a good job and wasted little time on anything else.

In Camus's book, Meursault, his principal character, is sentenced to death for shooting a man he doesn't know. But, more subtly, we see that he is being persecuted for his inability to put on an acceptable social face, to experience normal feelings like love, and to conform to society's expectations. Meursault is a listless figure and his emotional detachment is reflected in the novel's opening sentence: "Mother died today, or maybe it was yesterday." The only intense feelings shown by Meursault are expressed when he confronts a priest shortly before his execution and insists that life is meaningless, as the story concludes. Abandoning hope soothes Meursault and becomes the culmination of his gradually awakening awareness after the murder.

Though Ivan Illyich and Meursault wound their way to a sense of peace with death, their self-alienation never became fully acceptable to me. When depression found me in my early thirties, it was as if all the unanswered questions and longings of my college years reemerged, leaping out to seize me like a troll that had been hiding under a bridge. Through this time, I recognized my soul's desire for wholeness as an urge coming from within, and I became determined to bring my life to a different conclusion than Meursault's lack of meaning.

* * *

When we view the word "stranger" through our mythic lens, it takes on a meaning very different from the existentialist notion of being cast into an indifferent world. In mythology, the stranger may be a mystery, god, devil, or angel in disguise. Zeus and Hermes arrived as strangers at the door of Baucis and Philemon. Carefully disguised to test humankind before the flood, they generously rewarded the old couple for their hospitality. In Greek mythology, to risk seeing a god undisguised was to risk death. However, when greeted in disguise, their services could range from lover to seer. In the Western tradition, Jacob awakened to a night-long fight for his life with a stranger who turned out to be an angel. Abraham and other religious figures had many encounters with angels who showed up initially as strangers.

And in psychological terms, the stranger signifies a part of us that is still wandering in our unconscious, often repressed and unassimilated from the path of personal identification.

The stranger is a personification of part of our shadow, which represents all the attributes we could have brought into our identity but did not. In reaction to our early environment, we have cut these attributes out of our conscious life, yet they remain with us, partly repressed and unlived. Paradoxically, our shadow may hold along with our darker qualities some of our most positive potentials. But our family, education, society, and other influences led us to reject or repress them during our early development.

We have two fundamental components in our identity. The first, as I've previously discussed, is our ego, our conscious sense of "I." The second is our shadow, the unconscious *stranger* within us. This duality in our personality forms one of the most significant areas of Jungian thought relating to projection, which I previously introduced. Projection is the mechanism by which we first become aware of our latent potentials. It is the outward, unconscious displacement of something originally located within our personality. When we take our projection back, even if it is negative, we enlarge our personality and transform it.

For example, when a young woman, Gina, first consulted me I soon realized she had buried part of herself. Gina's father was the dean of students at a small Southern college. Her mother spent her life as a "faculty wife," while nurturing a secret rage that she hadn't gone to medical school.

Gina had been drawing as long as she could remember, and her only desire was to become an artist. While her parents loved to show off her paintings and drawings, they totally opposed her ambitions. Her father took the position that being a studio artist was a financially insecure, impractical way of life. Her mother urged Gina to join the legions of smart women who were breaking down Old Guard barriers and train for a profession. Both of Gina's parents felt the artist's life was morally disreputable, filled with wanton sex, drugs, and alcohol.

Needless to say, these were heavy shadow projections on their part. Their fear and rigidity had caused them to repress their own sexuality, creativity, passion, and inspiration in favor of a "sensible" life. The life of an artist represented the antithesis of all they stood for.

Gina's adolescence and most of her college years were spent in a depression and bouts of promiscuity, a compulsion to act out her parents' worst fears. She graduated from law school but never practiced. She continued to paint as a "hobby." After two failed marriages and a series of mediocre jobs, she suddenly found that she was unable to paint anymore. Frozen with fear, she began to feel panicky at the very thought of painting. Though she had felt for a long time that she had betrayed the truest part of herself, she now believed it was too late to change. Nothing is so bleak as losing one's desire for life. Almost two years of analytic work were required before she could unlock her "inner artist" and value it appropriately.

As we adapt socially, we often learn to repress the parts of ourselves that have a capacity to be openly sensuous and loving, along with our capacity to be fierce or violent. As I noted earlier, we usually take these rejected, repressed aspects of ourselves and project them onto other people and groups. When she was in college, Gina, an artist at heart, lived out her parents' shadow projection.

Gina's experience is evidence of the split between our ego and our shadow—between who we think we are and who we are convinced we are not. Becoming aware of this inner split is the first step toward self-knowledge and the foundation of true psychological development.

Usually we are confronted with this reality when life seems to be conspiring against us—when our vitality has dried up, illnesses beset us, and our values seem to have turned on us. Such times are terrifying and depressing because we believe we have lost the ground that supports us. Life is uncertain; the perspectives of church, family, society, or whatever represents our central values appear to be under attack and in danger of fragmenting. We feel inadequate and out of control.

But the confrontation also brings with it a personal, compelling need for wholeness. Waking up to our own reality seems to open a door through which life can become more than we could have imagined. If we don't walk through the door, we will pay a price in terms of our health, our relationships, and our vitality.

Society's Shadow

We must realize that if we fail in our individual development, our failures will be reflected in the development of the society we make up. Likewise, our society's problems in health care, crime, poverty, unemployment, and education are issues that reflect human values and will continue until we learn to regard the person more highly than economics or efficiency. Learning to recognize and deal with our personal and collective shadow is the key to regaining a sense of balance and opportunity, for ourselves as well as our culture.

Harry Stack Sullivan, the founder of Interpersonal Psychiatry, would begin his opening lecture to psychiatric residents by saying, "I am an alcoholic, I am a homosexual, I am a schizophrenic." By making this statement he faced the potentials in his shadow by bringing them into the light. Dr. Sullivan clearly wanted the young doctors to understand that all human potentials—including the socially unacceptable ones—live in each of us. He understood that to work well with others to bring healing, we must be able to find their shadow potentials within our own psyches—and listen to what they have to say.

I believe that psychological maturity begins when we know that every positive attribute of our personality has a potential dark side, and that, conversely, every negative attribute has a potential positive or bright aspect. The paradox of the shadow is that what appears to be manure may actually be excellent fertilizer, and a wounded past or dark present may be a call to a promising future.

Just as we are capable of personal shadow projections, we often project negative or "evil" qualities onto other societies, particularly those very different from our own. For example, seeing communism as an "evil empire" was a societal shadow projection. Currently we are engaged in a large shadow struggle in the Middle East. We have projected our shadow onto countries that don't seem to value democracy and capitalism and that are governed by religious fervor and conservatism. At the same time it is clear that many Middle Eastern groups that support terrorism see us as the "Great Satan" that will destroy their values and culture. They, likewise, have projected their shadow onto the United States. Within our own society, too, we project much of our collective shadow onto minority groups, leading to racism and anti-Semitism. If our society has any hope of breaking this pattern and evolving into a more conscious form, we must first recognize that we are making collective projections and then begin the process of recollecting, or taking them back.

* * *

As a child I was very shy and found myself particularly intimidated by my father's ability to think fast and enjoy speaking in public. For years I was either envious of or irritated by people who seemed to speak easily in front of groups. Gradually I have been able to find this ability within myself, but only after I realized I was engaging in projection. People who have repressed their anxiety may become exasperated with someone who appears very nervous. The person reminds them of their own hidden feelings and tends to open the door to them. But when they see someone who is cool under stress, they will admire him or her. In a different situation, those who have repressed strong feelings of inferiority may find themselves unreasonably angry with another person who is more dominating. Secretly, however, they may be jealous of the person's ability to take charge of a situation.

In these cases we can see that a past wound to our identity may cause us to be afraid of a painful emotion or public embarrassment. We will meet people who will trigger these disowned parts of ourselves, like fun house mirrors reflecting our feelings and inadequacy and longing. But the emotion we experience, especially when it is strong, should remind us to look deeper within.

Projection is like looking at the world through dirty glasses and not being able tell whether the streaks you see are on your lenses or part of the landscape. We see others through the glasses of our own reactions, then read into them qualities that are really in ourselves. The faults I most severely criticize, like the qualities I most admire, are usually pointers to something within me.

In another example, after her first few weeks of analysis Kathy told me her sister-in-law had made her feel insignificant at a family gathering when she criticized her sensual and fashionable dress. Kathy lay awake that night for hours, arguing her case and proving that her sister-in-law had been out of line. Round and round the arguments continued in her head until suddenly she heard a voice saying, "The defendant has admirably stated the case for her own prosecution."

Kathy told me that she sat up startled. Then she began to think about our discussion on the shadow. She realized that on another occasion she had behaved in exactly the same way her sister-in-law had. In other words she had the capacity to make belittling remarks, especially when she was feeling anxious or worried about her own appearance. With this fresh insight, her resentment evaporated. She had withdrawn her projection, stopped reading her own fault into the other woman, and discovered a bruised spot in her own personality she needed to heal. She soon fell into a peaceful sleep.

Remember that recollecting our projections involves much more than just having an awareness of them. We must also develop an awareness of their double aspects, representing the split within our personality that we must learn how to bridge.

Jolande Jacobi, an analyst and colleague of Jung, says,

> For example, an alcoholic, in order to be cured, must not only be conscious of his tendency or compulsion to drink—which many of them deny—but must also discover the deeper reasons that have induced his craving. These reasons are always shadow qualities which he cannot accept, which he flees from in order to rid himself of the pangs of conscience their recognition would entail. The precondition for a cure, therefore, is that the alcoholic

should keep these shadow qualities constantly before him, seeing in his mind's eye this drinker in himself as his unswerving companion, until he can no longer forget his presence.

In this case, the alcoholic within us that takes over our personality isn't just a destructive force. It is also a message that we must change our lives. It is telling us that the way we are living is killing us. Whether we drink for fun, escape, relaxation, a release from fear, inner drivenness, inner criticism, guilt or something else, we need to look inward to find our woundedness and the authentic potentials we have been unable to live.

To fulfill this task means taking on our greatest weakness as our greatest teacher until we are totally transformed. As I pointed out earlier, this transformation means death to our old personality and way of life. In many cases the supportive, structured help of a group such as Alcoholics Anonymous is useful in the face of such a daunting task.

In integrating new aspects of our shadows, our dreams can frequently help us. Our shadow characteristics are often personified in our dreams as people of the same sex as us. Sometimes we may resist them when we realize they represent aspects of our shadow that can be dangerous to our well-being; sometimes we have to give them compassion and love. Only when they are ignored or misunderstood will these aspects of ourselves almost always become hostile to our later development.

The Shadow and Development

Developing knowledge of the shadow is immensely important because the shadow stands between our ego and our Self. In religious terms, it stands between us and our relationship with the Divine. We can see why the ancient spiritual guides in Christian mysticism referred to the first stage of the journey toward their relationship with the Divine as "the purgative way." In this stage, the pilgrim's task was to struggle to confront the obstacles in him- or herself—

the attitudes, habits, and beliefs that hindered the journey toward realizing the spiritual world. However, this ancient forerunner to what, in psychological terms, we call working on our shadow often focused on eliminating negative qualities but failed to see the positive and energetic potential many of them had, once understood and transformed by self-awareness.

The most important awareness we gain upon learning about our shadow is that, in an important way, we are strangers to ourselves. And in many ways, we are strangers to our spiritual and sexual potentials. Our wholeness is divided and our desire is subject to unknown forces. Our shadow may urge us to give up in the face of adversity or compel us to go on, regardless of what we "think" we want. It may represent the spirit of our unlived potential that we fearfully try to deny, or it may represent the self-hate we carefully hide. Whatever it is, our shadow is wholly other and opposite from who we think we are—and is more emotionally powerful than we know.

Here is another example of the shadow at work. A very exact and meticulous man, who had difficulty showing anger, mailed but neglected to sign his alimony checks for several months in a row. He refused to believe he could make such a mistake until he was confronted with the evidence by his wife's attorney. As you've probably guessed, he was still harboring feelings of anger toward her, especially about her lack of desire for him when they were married. However, he had never expressed this anger and always explained what a wonderful person his former wife was, how smooth their divorce proceedings had been, and how they were still friends. His conscious self truly believed everything positive he was saying, while without his being aware of the fact, his shadow was angry, busy sabotaging his relationship with her. In other words he was denying his split feelings and repressing the ones that threatened the image of reality he wanted to believe. Our feelings and our actions are complicated, but we rarely spend the time necessary to identify them. When we do this, we will understand how our shadow is actually controlling our life.

The fact that we project our shadow onto other people and

misconstrue their nature doesn't mean there aren't some truly evil people in the world. It simply means we need to be aware of Jung's admonition that "much that proves to be abysmally evil in its ultimate effects does not come from man's wickedness, but from his stupidity and unconsciousness." Jung's emphasis here is on the importance of our undertaking a rigorous examination of ourselves so *we* will stop creating evil people in the world. Until we come to know the shadow aspects of ourselves, we will project them onto others and thereby help to create the terrible situations that we find exist.

This subject is very complex. We may believe that we don't create evil people (or stupid/unconscious people), that they are really and incontrovertibly there. If we project our inner hatred onto some group like the skinheads or KKK, it doesn't mean they are not in reality hate mongering or that we are making them into hate mongers. But it does mean that if I have an extreme emotional reaction to them, I am seeing myself in them without realizing it. My emotional reaction has to do with what is going on in *me*, and in terms of my development, I need to understand what is being disclosed about my personality.

If enough of my "group" projects its shadow onto a small group, that group can feel powerless and disenfranchised. They may turn to terrorism in an effort to be recognized and dealt with. To some extent, we have then created terrorists. One can imagine, for instance, that this was the case with Libya; in the 1970s Libya tried to be friends with the United States, and we laughed at them and rejected their efforts as they hired President Carter's brother as a lobbyist. Or we could imagine that the militia movement within our country represents the shadow of many of us, as we have let our government become controlled by big money and institutional interests at the expense of valuing individual citizens. Closer to home, in our families and workplaces, we have a lot more to do with creating our adversaries than we realize. Our failure to understand and acknowledge individual differences, especially those that threaten us because they represent our hidden selves, is an endless source of conflict that saps our energy and drains our self-esteem.

If we remain unconscious, repressing our shadow characteristics and projecting them onto other people apparently has certain advantages. We are able to rid ourselves of painful inner conflicts by passing them on to someone else and thereby protecting our self-image. Then we can blame someone else or some external circumstance for our problems. Our task, however, is to look through the outer layer of our experience and into its inner meaning. Should we fail in this task, we will meet our inner conflicts as fate in our outer lives.

If Kathy hadn't realized the projection she was placing on her sister-in-law, they might have quarreled continuously. The bad blood between them could have polarized their family, forcing its members to choose sides and endure years of coldness and hostility. No one could have predicted how difficult and harmful this conflict might have become had it been acted out and spread.

However, whether within our psyche or without, we need the stranger. Elie Wiesel, whose experiences in German concentration camps burned into his soul the meaning of being a stranger and an object of projection, writes that "a society without strangers would be impoverished; to live only amongst ourselves, constantly inbreeding, never facing an outsider to make us question again and again our certainties and rules, would inevitably lead to atrophy. The experience of encountering a stranger—like the experience of suffering—is important and creative, provided we know when to step back."

Ancient cultures knew the power and complexity of strangers and adopted elaborate rituals of courtesy towards them. This is because in Greek mythology, as I mentioned, the stranger may have been a god in disguise. In the Christian tradition, the stranger may be Christ appearing as one of the "least of these." In this same tradition, Christ was born as a stranger to the conventional world of politics, power, and orthodoxy. The typical Christmas scene depicts this paradox by showing the Christ child's birth in a stable. And though he was greeted by angels, wise men and shepherds, his birth was seen as a threat to conventional authority. Such rituals ease our fear that comes from facing the unknown.

The Judaic tradition instructs us to love God with all of our heart, to love our neighbor as ourselves, and to love the stranger. However, it doesn't encourage loving them *naively*. The accumulated wisdom of this tradition recognizes that some kinds of strangers are dangerous and must be resisted. And it considers the most destructive strangers to be persons who appear to be one of us, but are not, and who use their neighbors' faith in them to do harm.

Within our soul the stranger represents a question that challenges our certainties and forces us to re-examine our lives, our values, our actions, and, in general, who we think we are. Such questions may expand or even explode our boundaries, but if our shadow attempts to *force* answers and behaviors on us we must resist it. An extreme example of such a situation can be found in multiple personality disorder. In these cases a stranger or strangers take over the personality because the person's ego is too wounded, weak, or fragmented to reject it. Often these strangers represent a potential for transformation, but we need to be careful and be sure we remember that the support of another strong, experienced person is necessary until we find out the stranger's intentions and potentials, otherwise we may become overwhelmed. I have known other people who have become severely depressed simply by reflecting upon an intense dream image.

Meeting Our Shadow

As I have touched on, our dreams are one of the easiest ways to get to know our shadow. It is as if they are the chapel where the conscious and unconscious dimensions of our soul can wed. Not long ago, I was working with Richard, a successful gentleman who had a dream in which a shadow figure appeared as "evil," then later turned out to be enlightenment in disguise. Richard had achieved a position of prominence in his profession and in the community. This able and distinguished man had many admirable qualities, including intelligence, industry, courage, and determination. He served on various boards in his community and as an elder in his church. He was married to a lovely, intelligent, modestly wealthy woman with whom he had three children, who were now in early adulthood. For several years he and his wife had lived privately apart in their spacious house, but in public they stood united for the sake of appearance.

The only visible blemish on the face of this family was their youngest daughter, who had a continuous drug problem. Their friends were sympathetic and wondered how this situation could happen in such a fine family. Most thought it was just a sign of the times. This problem, and Richard's depression over it, is what finally brought him to my office. I was charmed by Richard's courteous manner and elegant appearance. His wife, however, was no longer charmed by him and had accused him of being less than a man. Because he had never felt much sexual desire and now seemed to feel none at all, he was afraid she was right. After a few months in analysis Richard said,

> I dreamed I was in an expensive shopping area. There were stores like Saks Fifth Avenue and Tiffany's. I was looking in the window of an elegant store full of exquisite clocks. In the store window I saw the reflection of an old, seedy-looking man. He had on a very unkempt suit, and I thought he must be a sexual pervert. He then moved close behind me and stood touching me and rubbing against me.
>
> I quickly left and later stopped in front of a beautiful jewelry store. Again I saw his reflection as he moved up against me. He began caressing me. I dashed into the store and called the police, screaming, "There is a pervert after me." Fortunately, they were close by and grabbed him. As they dragged him away he looked into my eyes. His face was filled with sorrow and he said, "You poor, poor fool."

"When I awoke," Richard continued, "I felt repulsed that this person might actually be a part of me. And yet I felt I had made a mistake by calling the police."

I agreed with him that what was represented in the dream by his calling the police probably did point to an attitude in his waking life that did not ultimately serve him. He said, "But isn't that what anyone would do?"

I suggested Richard write out an imaginary dialogue with the seedy man, asking him his name and why he had entered Richard's dream.

Richard needed several weeks to muster up the courage, but when he did so, the seedy man replied, "My name is Aware. I am your conscious awareness, and I'm trying to get your attention. You spend all of your time living in beautiful, expensive fantasies of life, and you act as if it's an act of perversion to face your own reality."

In order to maintain appearances, Richard had denied reality, banished the truth from his relationships, and was living a fantasy life. Indeed, he had put most of his vitality into his career at the expense of learning to develop his capacities for eros and relationship. Now a frightening inner figure, if properly understood, was offering him the key that could unlock the door to a whole new approach to life.

Richard's dialogues with Aware went on for several months, building new wholeness into his life. Through his inner work he uncovered even more of his shadow. He found the strength to be less courteous, to be more demanding of his family and able to become involved with the kind of confrontations with himself, his daughter, and his wife that were to become transforming. He found some of the anger he had been repressing, as well as his sexual desire. Richard began to understand that life, when lived with strength and integrity, doesn't always looks so tidy and polished. Closing his eyes to reality was no longer an option for him.

This example suggests that what we generally fear most about strangers is that they may force us to see ourselves in ways that don't fit into our cherished view. The threatening or repulsive intruder is, in fact, a common dream motif. The intruder may be a burglar, a tramp, a salesperson, a political or religious figure, or some other person we may be inclined to regard with suspicion. We will fear this outsider and try desperately to shut out or avoid him or her. Yet when we contact and dialogue with the person, he or she will usually turn out to be helpful.

As we have seen, many examples of myths and legends can teach us as well as dreams and psychological theory. One of my favorites is about St. Francis and the wolf. In this story, set in Italy long ago when forests were vast, some local village people began to notice that their chickens and livestock were disappearing. Soon an occasional child or older person would be missing. The villagers realized that a ferocious wolf had moved into the nearby woods.

While animals and weaker people were its customary prey, the wolf seemed to fear no one. The villagers tried in vain to poison, capture, or kill it but were unsuccessful. They called upon hunters from near and far to help. Elegant noblemen with great horses, packs of hounds, and many retainers responded, but the wolf managed to evade them all.

Finally the village elders, in desperation, sent a message to St. Francis imploring his help in getting rid of the beast. St. Francis came immediately to their aid. He set out for the wolf's lair, deep into the forest, perhaps farther than anyone had gone before. There he found the wolf. They stood before each other eye to eye, for some time, then St. Francis said simply, "Brother Wolf."

When St. Francis returned to the village, the villagers gathered around him in great excitement and begged him to tell them how to deal with the wolf.

He said to them, "Feed your wolf."

For many of us our childhood wounds, lost potentials, and the shadow figures representing our self-alienation are our personal wolves. So are our denied passions, sexual and spiritual. We cannot successfully repress them or pray them away. Neither can we banish them with willpower, grieve or heal them away. To lose them is to lose ourselves, for they are part of our souls, necessary for our wholeness. We must face them, make them brothers or sisters, and feed them. In other words, we must come into conscious relationship with them.

* * *

The perspective on the shadow and on projections that I've presented here illustrates the paradoxes that are part of this important work and the difficulty of fulfilling the desires of our soul. This perspective also shows that our inner world and our outer world are always connected with a dynamic tension that calls us to explore and adapt to both of them as their realities unfold in our experience. Further, we can see that the ancient traditions outlining careful ways to treat strangers embodied a wisdom on a level higher than that of our contemporary, mechanical, and often one-dimensional approach to life, a wisdom on the more fluid level of vital experience. Our ancient forebears knew these rituals weren't just meant to protect strangers. They were also meant to protect us from ourselves.

Fear and Delight

The truths revealed in myths, stories, and dreams remind us of the value of metaphors and other symbols, which reflect a variety of personal meanings. Father Andrew Greeley, the co-author of *The Bible and Us,* points out: "It is in the nature of metaphor to startle and shock, to destroy old patterns of perceptions with surprising new insight that we then integrate into a revised and more illuminated pattern of perception."

Metaphors can result in a moment of terror, as our conventional structures of thought and feeling are immediately turned upside down. (The pervert in the dream challenged a distinguished man's view of himself and seemed to validate one of his deepest fears.) But metaphors can also bring moments of delight, for once our old structures have crashed, we feel a sense of relief. Though we may still feel threatened by seeing both sides of ourselves, this knowledge can bring a new sense of authenticity and freedom into our lives. When, for example, the depression that caused my career change became a teacher, I was terrified. It was telling me that the path I had worked so hard to follow was leading to destruction. But once I realized this fact, I slowly began to feel new hope and then finally excitement at the prospect of a new, more genuine approach to life.

Delight begins when we can see or experience the illumination and the creativity that metaphor brings. Suddenly, new answers and new ways of perceiving and living stand open before us—as Richard discovered when he found that long-lost, valuable—but not entirely pleasant—part of himself. Likewise, the story of St. Francis meeting the wolf, claiming it as a brother and telling the villagers to "feed their wolf" evokes a sense of delight. Isn't it joyful that a metaphor instructs us to feed our own capacity to be wild and fierce?

We often wonder why life has to be so complicated and difficult. The straightforward answer is that our nature is this way; we learn by shocks and surprises. As in the story in which the Pharaoh refused to accept change and let Moses and his people go, or in the story of Herod after the birth of Jesus, who in fear of the loss of future power slaughtered all of the newborn baby boys in Bethlehem, so do our egos prefer to hold onto old attitudes until we are shocked out of them. Our own nature and the nature of life are such that paradox and metaphor are some of the best ways we have of getting that shock.

Taking this work seriously requires an amount of personal sacrifice. In order to give energy to our inner world, we must take time from our busy lives to listen to the whispering of our Self, through our dreams or as they are expressed in the voices of our complaints and resentments. These negative feelings have their own value that can offer as much to life as positive feelings do. Such a sacrifice doesn't require willpower. It requires desire—a desire for a richer, deeper life so strong that it will move us to put these values foremost in our hearts.

Chapter 8

TRANSFORMING TO HEAL SOCIETY

Nearly all great civilizations that perished did so because they had crystallized, because they were incapable of adapting themselves to new conditions, new methods, new points of view. It is as though people would literally rather die than change.

—ELEANOR ROOSEVELT, TOMORROW IS NOW

Meursault, Camus's protagonist in *The Stranger,* reflected the psychological condition of a twentieth-century man who found himself awakening emotionally in a world dominated by rationality. It was a world where logos had lost its ground in philosophy and in its partnership with mythos. A world where desire and soul were estranged. Rationality alone leaves us abandoned in a spiritual desert once it has drained the meaning from love and a culture's customs. It turns everything we love into an illusion. Mythos, on the other hand, reminds us that life is a journey, love is central to that journey, and the journey is purposeful, even holy.

The ancient Greeks honored logos and mythos in philosophy and religion. The descendants of Abraham founded religions in which the two were intertwined. By the Middle Ages, local religious life offered systems of understanding human life and transformation, such as the rituals of the mass and other religious services. Whatever their limitations, the mosque, church, and temple offered communal and time-tested practices designed to promote social ethics, teach caring for each other, mediate a relationship with the Divine, and gradually transform one's character.

Religious customs and ceremonies were part of local and national life and facilitated living a life guided by the soul's inspiration. They punctuated the rhythms of public life with regular periods of community-wide reflection, celebration, and remembrance. Every week took its shape in the stillness of Saturday's Sabbath or Sunday morning's confessional and mass. The beginning of autumn brought the Days of Atonement to Jews as regularly as the darkest period of winter brought Christmas to Christians and spring delivered celebrations of new life. In monasteries, every hour of the day was ritualized, ordered, and sacralized.

After the factory whistle began to drown out the church bells, however, office buildings towered over the steeples, and science cast a skeptical eye on the ordained word. Camus's Meursault found himself in a world no longer grounded in mythos. In this changed world, rhythm was based on productivity, not on the spiritual practices that had once helped one find order and meaning.

Like everyone else, I have been shaped by the times I live in. And I have discovered that if mythos is to become part of my experience, I have to develop it personally. I have to heal within myself society's wounds to the soul. "Personally" doesn't mean alone, for others are searching, too, including some of our finest thinkers. And the great themes of philosophy, religion, mythology, and literature are still here, waiting to help me as I study them within the context of my experience of life today.

The Art of Living

The author Pat Conroy tells us that the artist can turn the worst moment of his or her life into "something sweetly and untellably beautiful." This is the kind of transformation that can help each of us turn our suffering into what my wife and I call "creative suffering," which can help us love life in a way stronger than death, and find a new beginning in every ending.

Let's reconsider the story of Adam and Eve. As I interpreted earlier, it opens us to the idea of Eternal Beginnings. It is also the first step of an archetypal pilgrimage, the pilgrimage of human life. Psychologically, it symbolizes the necessity of leaving a state of unconscious dependency and fully entering the labors of life. Because this expulsion is archetypal, it is neither a mistake nor the result of improper living. The story is simply an illustration of Eternal Truth. And as an archetypal truth—happening now and always—it shows us that we will find ourselves continually beginning new aspects of life's journey.

Beginning steps are initiated by eros, by some kind of desire. This desire may be the love of a person, the love of an idea or a place, the wish for a more fulfilling life, or the relief from suffering that nature, "fate," our prior actions, or our view of life has backed us into. For example, as a result of his encounter with cancer and paraplegia, the writer Reynolds Price discovered that he had been forced into a whole new life, one that was deeper, more personal, and more creative than his former life had been. He shares that journey with us in his book, *A Whole New Life*.

The word "desire" descends from the Latin word *desiderare*, which means to long for or to await what the stars will bring. With this in mind, let's look at another mythological meaning of the serpent: the desire that heals and renews life. Because it sheds its skin, it is also a symbol of Eternal Becoming. Because it is close to the earth, it symbolizes an instinctual nature that longs for the future (and as part of desire, sexual yearnings also call forth the future). The dark side of the serpent symbol can be destructive, but it is a destruction that begins the transformational process of birth, life, death and rebirth. Thus symbolically the snake tells the story of creation and transformation, which relates on the individual level to initiation into the mysteries of life and the resulting unfolding spiral of conscious development.

Like the snake, the legendary apple (commonly thought of as being the "fruit" of the Tree of Knowledge of Good and Evil, though no specific fruit is actually named in the Bible) is an old friend to mythologists. In folklore, the red apple symbolizes knowledge of the heart that leads to wholeness, but a knowledge that hasn't yet been redeemed. In the mystical tradition of Judaism, the fruit of the other tree in the garden, the Tree of Life, is the golden apple; it symbolizes the ultimate fruit of life, or, in psychological terms, redeemed consciousness. I believe that all the parts of the Tree of Life are related in harmony—upper and lower, masculine and feminine. The basic split between the Tree of Knowledge and the Tree of Life is a split between knowledge and life. We must eat the apple of knowledge and digest it until it is absorbed and metabolized into the act of living. The redness of an apple, the deep color of blood, reminds us that knowledge means to live a life through our heart as well as our mind.

The story of Adam and Eve represents a call to leave whatever state we have become bogged down in and return to one where vitality is possible, where we have to meet life, love, and ourselves face to face and become larger in spirit and consciousness than we were before. Perhaps this is one of the biblical meanings of God's love—that we can follow his example and journey into life realizing that this call may bring suffering, but it is not a punishment. These deeper reflections can help revitalize the meaning of our religious heritage and help heal our religious institutions.

The Faces of Transformation

Jung refers to the spiritual and psychological journey of development as the "individuation process." This journey leads toward the self-realization of our entire personality. The true goal of life—this comprehensive development of ourselves—lasts to the very end of our lives and supersedes the goal of a shallow sense of "happiness." Our journey toward wholeness gives our lives incomparable value, a value centered in an inner life, which can never be lost. It is greater than many other more transient values that our culture endorses. The lives of Christ and the biblical prophets, of rulers, apostles and saints, as well as the lives of Buddha and other major religious figures all illustrate this point.

Individuation requires continual personal transformation. And as we transform, our society also transforms. Jung, in fact, believed that meaningful social change could *only* be the result of individual changes coming together and transforming a social group.

This transformational process—birth, life, death and rebirth—reflects the cycles of nature; we see it around us in the seasons and in plant life—birth in spring, blossoming in summer, decline in fall, death in winter, and renewal the following spring. Our ancient forebears realized that this cycle was a metaphor for our own development, the "Wheel of Life"—the process that is constantly going on within us.

The fact that I am always becoming is literally true. I am not the same as I was when I began this sentence, biologically, emotionally or mentally. Many, many small changes have taken place and are taking place within me. As I am part of nature, the idea that my psychological and spiritual development follows nature's designs, and reflects eternal and archetypal patterns, is a natural conclusion.

In ancient mythology this pattern is exemplified in the hero's quest. This quest, whether for man or woman, requires that one leave the everyday world, at least in spirit, and descend to the underworld to find the treasure that can renew life. I took this metaphorical journey during my Dionysian year in college, where the seeds were sown for the future, and again during my depression in my early thirties and a number of times since. From the standpoint of Jungian psychology, the underworld symbolizes the collective unconscious, the home of our archetypal patterns and elemental truths—the depth of our soul, where we find renewal and the sparks of new life. After finding the treasure, the hero then makes an ascent, returning to the ordinary world of life and enriching it with his or her discovery and thus wedding outer life with inner depth. The mythic pattern is that of descent/treasure/ascent, in symbolic parallel with life/death/rebirth.

Jung clearly believed that these patterns of transformation continued to occur throughout our lives. He then wondered if there was a general configuration to show how they occur, and found the answer in his studies of alchemy. This medieval chemical science and philosophy was aimed at transmuting base metals into gold, discovering a universal cure for disease, and indefinitely prolonging life.

Jung believed that alchemists projected their internal psychological processes—their individuation process—into what they were doing. As they carried out their various operations, they enjoyed deeply passionate emotional and spiritual experiences, even though they never literally succeeded in reaching their goals. They wrote at length about their soul's journeys. In studying their ancient manuscripts, two things become clear. First, they did not attempt to split their experiences from their activity; second, as they proceeded, the "process" of their work became more important to them than its outcome. Their work was to transform base metals into something more valuable, usually gold. They also aimed to transform matter into spirit, thus creating the elixir of life or the philosopher's stone. The various goals of the alchemists may be seen as metaphors for a consistent effort to create a life of personal value, spiritual meaning, and fulfillment.

In alchemy, the symbolic formula for the cycle of transformation is base material/dissolution/coagulation. If I had applied this metaphor to my personal life when I was a young man, the base material of my experience of living would have been restlessness and depression. The emotional "heat" of my disturbances led me into therapy, where the base material began to dissolve. My personal psychology was consequently transformed so that it "coagulated" or came together in a way that expressed a new level of self-understanding and purpose in life closer to my true nature. As a symbolic process, this formula describes our inner search for psychological and spiritual completion.

The alchemists' primary material is dense and heavy, like lead. This symbolically relates to a heaviness of heart or spirit, often reflected in symptoms such as anxiety, depression, weight problems, addictions, feelings of inertness, worthlessness, and so on. Heat is applied to this matter, forcing it to dissolve. This means, as I noted in my own example, that our condition becomes so emotionally or symptomatically painful that we seek help and a process of transformation begins. When the heat is removed, it coagulates into a new form. This indicates symbolically that as the painful symptoms are worked through and understood, new possibilities for living begin to form. In mythological terms, the world of fire that produces heat is the world of original emotional experience. It represents the hero's quest to face the trials of life. As Joseph Campbell points out, this seeking will thus "bring a whole new body of possibilities into the field of interpreted experience for other people to experience. . . ." This approach returns mythos or symbolic meaning to the healing process and transforms it to one of growth.

We would be mistaken, however, to think that the individuation process, or a relationship with the Self, will make life easy or full of happiness. But this relationship will be a rebirth, and it will give us a feeling of true and lasting security as a result of knowing that we have become grounded in our own being. From a spiritual point of view, we will have come into contact with the Divine in our daily existence, releasing the self-renewing force of passionate inner transformation. In this process, not only are we learning to serve our Self, we are also transforming our culture.

* * *

Much of modern psychology views the transformation process as one of organization/fragmentation/re-integration. However, most conventional therapists are unaware of the deeper dimensions of this process as they try to relieve suffering and return people to "normal." As a result, transformation may become blocked, leaving their clients trapped in a cycle they cannot complete. What usually follows is a deep dissociation in the suffering person's personality, as it splits off and devalues the part of itself that is seeking new life. This split results in an experience filled with despair and self-alienation.

Let us return once again to Fred, the contractor who had been depressed for several years. As you may remember, Fred was professionally successful and had a good family life. But he was stuck in his midlife transition. Fred's psychiatrists, with the best intentions, were treating his depression but not realizing what was behind it. They wanted to get him back to "normal." But they were only treating the symptoms without investigating their deeper meaning.

Fred's three years of conventional therapy almost destroyed him. His hospitalization cost him a lot of money, damaged his business and reputation, and terrified his family. This treatment that "didn't work" increased his feeling of despair and self-hate. If Fred hadn't run into an acquaintance who told him there was another possibility, in this case Jungian analysis, he might have continued on the same path until his depression became so severe as to be self-destructive. In that scenario, his fate would have been a misunderstood transformation that was acted out literally, rather than participated in psychologically. An aborted transformation almost always results in a death to our potentials. A completed transformation also involves a symbolic death, a death to our old way of living. But when we become stuck in the process because it is misunderstood, suicide may become an actual danger and an end to all possibilities of psychological renewal.

Conventional religious perspectives run the same risks when they fail to realize that the themes of all great spiritual traditions have been transformation, the sacrifice or death of an old way of life, and rebirth into a new way. Contemporary religions have far too commonly relied on emotionally based "conversion," a momentary catharsis that seems authentic but avoids the genuine process of transformation. A true conversion to a new way of life requires much more effort and commitment than an emotionally inspired moment.

Fred had been raised as a Roman Catholic and continued to practice this faith. His priest's response to Fred's ordeal was sympathetic. He offered his support and prayers, hoping Fred would recover as soon as possible. But the priest never considered that Fred might be having a spiritual crisis, a "dark night of the soul," during which he could have received support from the tradition, ritual, and symbolism of his religion.

One of the major differences between humans and other life forms is that we consciously experience our transformation. We experience it emotionally, which is often frightening, painful, and intense. When this begins, it is immensely helpful to understand that we are participating in a universal pattern. This knowledge can give us hope and reassurance that we are not alone in our experiences of life. The same is true for society. Understanding that our culture must also be transforming can give us hope for the future rather than simply scare us back into conservatism and fundamentalism. Religion and psychology are the only disciplines that deal with the emotional components of these experiences and their implications, and they need to include a depth perspective when looking at society, as well as individuals.

Jungian analyst Edward Edinger has spent decades studying the metaphors of mythology and religion from ancient Greece through the development of Christianity. He has noted that as our religious perspective progressed from polytheism to monotheism, a new destiny unfolded for humankind, personally and collectively. In ancient Greece, polytheistic gods lived on Mt. Olympus and had no truly personal relationship with humanity. During that age in that part of the world, humans thought themselves generally destined for a tragic fate. As that era of history was closing, about a thousand years before the birth of Christ, the idea of a monotheistic spirit was evolving in Greek culture. This idea introduced the notion that all people could participate in the Divine essence. As a result, self-responsibility as a personal spiritual characteristic developed.

In his study of this period, Dr. Edinger notes that the evolution of monotheism reflects a change in humanity's consciousness. Our individual personality had, for the first time, a potential for wholeness and unity. Psychologically, we evolved past the point where our inner forces, reflected outwardly as gods and goddesses, could autonomously unleash their contradictory energies within us and propel us into a tragic fate. (The Greek dramas portrayed the tragic fate humanity experiences when compelled by unconscious forces it is incapable of comprehending.)

This new potential for wholeness had profound spiritual meaning as well. In the Judaic tradition, monotheism evolved along with God's involvement with humanity and creation; religion became a way to be intimately related to the creative force of life, not simply an impersonal victim of it. In his book *Ego and Archetype*, Edinger goes on to examine the metaphor of the cross of Christ as a paradigm for what we experience as we undergo the transformation process. He suggests that the cross represents the symbolic points where life's contradictions meet, especially those where secular reality and Eternal Reality encounter each other in conflict. He believes that the passion, suffering, death, and res-urrection of Christ can symbolize the path our emotions follow when we are going through the major transformation processes of individuation. Thus the image of Christ on the cross can be very helpful to us psychologically without diminishing its profound religious meaning.

This perspective takes on even greater meaning if we combine the psychological and the religious approach. We can make the image of Christ truly personal when we say, "The Divine knows how we suffer in everyday life." Psychologically, we can interpret this image as holding the tension inherent in our conflicted situ-ation while seeking to understand it in a way that will open and broaden our personality. In this way, we can trust the symbolic path that shows that our pain will be transformed into peace and the delight of new life. (The story of Buddha's development and those of other great religious figures illustrate similar symbolic patterns.) If we can let go of our need for shallow emotional self-preservation and enhancement, our hearts will become open to life. Only a heart open to life can experience true joy and serve values greater than oneself.

Further, the story of Christ contains two additional psycho-logical aspects. The path of transformation followed by Christ is not a simple, unconscious event. That choice, if it becomes *our* choice, requires our intentional participation; it is not a simple ethical imitation of the events in Jesus' life. It means obeying the voice of God (the Self) within and following it with the same devotion with which Christ followed the voice that guided him. The theologian and religious writer Hans Küng notes that "when the cross is set apart from copy [imitation] and precisely then, it is and remains a challenge to take up one's own cross, to go one's own way in the midst of the risks of one's own situation and uncertain of the future."

Küng also points out that "the Cross of Jesus remains the scandal, the sign that the barriers between the profane and the sacred are finally down." When the "laws" we live by are turned upside down in this encounter between profane and sacred, our sense of I—our ego—experiences the dark night of the soul that I've referred to—a bleak period when all the principles we trusted and built our lives on seem to be failing us, or in alchemical terms a period of *nigredo*, as the Jew Saul experienced after his blindness and before discovering his transformation into the Apostle Paul.

Individuation means we must make hard choices and difficult commitments that we are willing to follow with devotion. But we may be comforted by the symbolic fact that Christ and his identity were *transformed*, not lost. The same is true for us. We don't experience a reflexive destruction of our old selves but a transformation that is founded upon—but refines—all we have experienced before.

Society and Transformation

As I've noted, our society follows the same pattern of transformation that our lives follow. We can see that collectively we have become fragmented and polarized. The old order, our old social consciousness and dominant attitudes, seems to be in conflict with our current situation.

In fact, we are now in a state of heightened conflict with many shadow components of our society's personality. These reflect characteristics of our collective nature that have been denied, repressed, and suppressed for a long time. They are symbolized by groups in our society who are angry, often because they are disenfranchised: African-Americans, homosexuals, religious fundamentalists, skinheads, militiamen, anti-abortion activists, and many others. They are also symbolized by the aged, the poor, the infirm, the chronically physically ill, the mentally ill, and countless others. The first list includes groups who are in active conflict with society. The second list includes those in passive conflict. Together, they exist in numbers greater than we can deny, reminding us that our current approaches to problem solving that neglect the soul haven't worked. However, if we can relate to the shadow aspects these groups represent, we will discover that they know things about life and death we like to deny—that life can be messy, fragile, sometimes hopeless and out of control.

Our society's character structure is threatened and weak and is responding by refortifying itself through these different groups. Their call for recognition poses basic questions that we must face regarding who we are as individuals. And when their pleadings are ignored and turn to threats, it is a call for us—all of us—to cultivate a new level of mutual respect for our differences. Society's soul doesn't exist in a vacuum. We make it up. As we become more authentic, spiritually mature and psychologically aware, we can each transform culture like a stone thrown into a pond. Waves emanate from us as our presence gains in substance.

Collectively, however, we seem to be stuck in the process of transformation, and our society's subsequent disassociations and alienations are rapidly increasing. We experience fear on a daily basis—our children are afraid in their schools and our elderly are afraid to go for a walk outside. We fear the strangers on our streets because there are so many cases of random violence. Beneath the rational surface of our highly organized lives lurks a volcano of anger and fear. And it is no accident; it is a sign of this ongoing transformation. Many people are seeking new spiritual paths while others are looking for security behind the walls of fundamentalism; still others try to live in busy denial.

The condition of our communities reflects our overall resistance to successful psychological and spiritual transformation. It represents a failure of consciousness, a failure of true spiritual growth, now and in our recent past. In a dramatic series of five paintings titled "The Course of the Empire," the nineteenth-century artist Thomas Cole depicts the way a culture develops, peaks, and then disintegrates when conscious transformation fails and the culture becomes an unconscious victim of the cycle of transformation. The series begins with a painting of the savage or natural state and progresses to a pastoral state, then to one of flourishing success, pictured as a majestic city such as ancient Rome. Then the series moves to a picture of conflict and destruction and finally ends in a scene of desolation. In order to deal with our problems, we need to understand the meaning of what we are experiencing. We need to recognize that major transitions bring conflict and that new consciousness is only born as old values break down. We must let go of some of our ideas about how life "should be" if we are to live into the mystery of life as it *is*. Hope and new vitality thrive in proportion to our ability to birth a new consciousness and a new desire for a better world.

Chapter 9

THE STAGNATION OF DESIRE

The great principle of transformation begins through the things that are
lowest. Things . . . that hide from the light of day and
from man's enlightened thinking hold also
the secret of life that renews itself again and again.

—C. G. Jung, Modern Man in Search of a Soul

Most of us travel a long way in our lives from the point where we began. Some of us continue the process of becoming more spontaneous and creative every year, while others seem to become content and static in their lives. The novelist Gail Godwin speaks to this issue in what has become a well-known passage from her book, *The Finishing School.* She writes,

> Death is not the enemy; age is not the enemy. . . . But what we ought to fear is the kind of death that happens in life. It can happen at any time. You're going along, and then at some point, you congeal . . . . You solidify and from then on your life is doomed to be a repetition of what you have done before . . . . there are two kinds of people walking around on this earth. One kind, you can tell just by looking at them at what point they congealed into their final selves. It might be a very *nice* self, but you know you can expect no more surprises from it. Whereas the other kind keep moving, changing.

By intention or neglect, desire has stagnated in people who have congealed. When this happens, life begins to lose its soul.

When I began my journey years ago, I thought that now that I was on the path, I would never congeal. I looked forward to a life of continuous self-actualization and growth. That was a naive assumption. I have since discovered that because our personality grows by successive transformations, we are going to repeatedly congeal, which is the necessary death for a psychological rebirth into the future.

I have always liked the analogy of comparing our personality's evolution to the way a lobster outgrows its shell. As the lobster gets larger, the shell doesn't grow—our soul longs for growth but our personality doesn't want to change. Eventually the pressure of the lobster's growth begins to crack the shell, until the lobster is able to emerge from it. Then the lobster must live in a vulnerable condition until it can grow a new shell. A person who has congealed is like a lobster who refuses to leave the old shell. But, unlike lobsters, we have a choice.

* * *

By midlife the new shell I had begun to grow after my career change was strong and secure. I had grown, through many difficulties, into my new profession and had worked to create a family that I thought would be stable and fulfilling. But my inner turmoil was still growing, and my marriage turned sour as my life once again started to feel stale and empty. Desolation soaked into my blood and marrow.

One night I awakened with a start, aroused by a single image from a dream. In the dream a naked, starving woman was sitting in a straight chair. The chair was in the shadows of a damp prison cell whose only light came from a tiny barred window high above her head. I lay in the dark of my bedroom, picturing this scene again and again until finally I felt compelled to get up and write it down, carefully noting every detail, every shade and every nuance of her expression. While I hadn't yet realized it, the shell was cracking.

As I followed the line of thinking this dream led me into, I slowly became aware that the balance I had sought through psychology, my studies of Zen, religion and other spiritual practices had imprisoned my soul. I needed another radical change in attitude toward my life to free the desires deep within me.

It wasn't easy to think about leaving what I thought was a new shell, or to consider that I had become stuck again. I was unhappy about having to face my situation yet another time; I didn't realize it was the archetypal pattern of growth. Additionally, I was proud of my risk taking, growth, and success so far and was reluctant to step out of the place I had earned for myself. I was also tempted to solidify into an image of an admired and respected person—the image Gail Godwin termed a *nice* one. The dark side of this image was to see myself as noble, sacrificing myself to my psychotherapy clients and family, and it was seductive. We are devilishly creative in looking for ways to play it safe. Even my analyst lacked faith in the process taking place in my psyche and seemed unconvinced that I faced a further transformation. I had never felt so alone.

Throughout this period I remained haunted by the image of the woman in the cell—I began to see her as a symbol of my soul. I sketched her in my dream journal. I saw her face in my mind every day. I was convinced that if I didn't learn how to free her, I would have a heart attack or some other illness, that whatever yearning that was imprisoned would soon turn toxic.

Gradually a daring thought began to emerge in my psyche. I no longer wanted to be centered or balanced. These initial longings had perhaps come about only to balance the effects of my early life. Now I longed to be on fire with the love of life. The image of this poor starved woman helped me understand that my despair was my yearning passion that my ego wasn't yet strong enough, brave enough, to live. This awareness caused me to change analysts and eventually to move out of my old shell and to Zürich to study, where I became a Jungian analyst.

* * *

Unlived life becomes a destructive, irresistible force that works softly but powerfully for transformation. Whenever life becomes congealed, the serpent energy (desire and the longing for transformation) in our psyche begins to surface and cause what I earlier defined as neurotic suffering. When we become rigid, overly responsible, repressed and duty bound, sexual problems are likely to stand out in the array of other problems. As an expression of my inner turmoil, I was also experiencing a lack of sexual desire, which eventually helped me understand how much I needed a more passionate approach to life. Sexual problems are always a tip-off that something else major is going on. We have responded to this emergence with several decades of scientific studies, educational approaches, and a continuous flow of self-help books about sexual methods and techniques. A very small amount of this response has been helpful. But confronting sexual problems should really introduce us to the deeper questions we would usually like to avoid. And more often than not, just like we find with the disenfranchised segments of our society, our shadow aspects symbolically represent the disenfranchised aspects of ourselves.

When we encounter a stuck place in our development, it is often because we have become rigid. The more we have entrenched ourselves in particular beliefs and attitudes—both personal and social—the more we will think we have found the *right* course in life, the *right* ideals, and the *right* principles of behavior. As a result, we suppose these beliefs and attitudes are eternally valid; we make a virtue of clinging to them and of resisting change. But this seemingly natural perspective leaves the "becoming" nature of life locked and struggling in our unconscious. Intolerance and even fanaticism are liable to result as we fight desperately to validate and strengthen our positions, even while life endangers them—as it inevitably will.

Wendy was a chic, thirty-five-year-old CPA for a large firm. She was unmarried. She drove a BMW and owned a comfortable condo in a very stylish area. But she had a troubling, repetitive experience. Every day when she left her apartment, she encountered an old, wretched bag lady. Filthy and toothless, the woman held out a grimy hand for money every time Wendy passed her. Frequently, a pool of urine was at her feet. Wendy wished someone would make the woman go away but never had the courage to report her to the condominium complex management.

During an analytic session, we decided to pursue the meaning this woman evoked in Wendy as a psychological image. It turned out that she represented everything Wendy despised. Wendy was perfectionistic and compulsively sanitary. She couldn't live with anyone else because she was unable to tolerate the clutter. She didn't like sex because it was too messy. In fact, she didn't like her body from the waist down for the same reason. Wendy had succeeded in cutting herself off from many of the experiences of being alive, particularly those that had to do with desire. After all, real life, beginning with childbirth, is inevitably "messy."

If this poor old woman had appeared in a dream of Wendy's, she might have seen her as representing an aspect of Wendy's shadow that reflected how Wendy had cut herself off from life and perhaps reduced her feminine self to the state of a beggar. As a real-life psychological image, she helped Wendy in the same way a dream image could have done.

She still stands in front of Wendy's building, but now, having benefited from her new insight, Wendy greets her by name and feels concern for her, though the woman refuses to go to a shelter or other social agency. In my reflection, I wonder if she isn't a useful image for all of us, reminding us what our attitudes are doing to life and the feminine soul, the animating force that seeks life through us.

Societal Problems and Transformation

As I've previously stated, sexuality is not a problem to be solved. In the case of infidelity, for example, deeper questions must be faced and lived into that address not whether what happened was right or wrong but "what does it mean?" Invariably, it means the partners need to redirect their energies toward finding the value and meaning of their relationship, or more specifically the value and meaning of their individual lives.

Because of the powerful context it is embedded in, sexual desire becomes an expression of our relationship to ourselves and others. How we practice it reflects our spiritual view of ourselves, as well as how much we love or hate ourselves. If we love ourselves, our sexual expressions, even when strong, will take place in an atmosphere of love and respect. If we despise ourselves, our sexual activity will be degrading and practiced in ways that diminish our self-respect, our soul.

Sexuality either brings us into the struggles of life or forces us back into ourselves, hiding or denying our full humanity. Sometimes the pressure becomes so great that we need a period of celibacy to heal and find ourselves again. But in general, sexual issues are encouraging us into new situations, relationships, commitments, responsibilities, and opportunities. Understanding sexuality from the standpoint of mythos reveals its power in our lives, and teaches us to treat it with reverence and respect—that is, as something sacred.

The search for the meaning behind our sexual difficulties requires, as with the rest of our development, that we shift our emphasis from searching for *answers* to searching for deeper *questions*. Let's allow sexuality to transform us by doing our part—holding the tension of our dilemmas and opening our hearts. We must learn to accept the process of transformation as a challenge that requires a full and devoted response.

Marriage in our culture dramatically reflects both the symptoms of distress in our times and our efforts to transform the meanings embodied in an ancient tradition. For centuries our forebears viewed marriage as a social concern. In the Middle Ages, women were pawns, married off for family, political, and financial interests. Even in my generation, in the mid-twentieth-century, many women went to college to find a husband. And our religious institutions sanctified these marriages. As our more modern lives have evolved, ideas of love, romance, and fulfillment beyond social roles have also evolved. Marriage, as the traditional shell meant to contain and protect our relationships and families, has become too small. This shell has cracked, as evidenced by the number of divorces and new forms of relationships that are emerging. This fragmentation threatens many and rightfully frightens some social commentators. But we must learn how to participate in the transformation process and endure its tensions. By experiencing the instability of our struggling, it can then be reborn into something new.

* * *

Brian and Joyce had been married for almost twenty-eight years, since late adolescence. When Joyce phoned me for an appointment, her voice was so choked with emotion she could barely speak. After months of badgering, Joyce's suspicions were confirmed when Brian confessed to having been involved with another woman for over a year. Joyce felt shattered. She had given up a career to raise her children, and she now found herself wondering if she had thrown her life away.

Brian, at the same time, was filled with shame and remorse. While he couldn't understand what had possessed him, he confessed to me that the affair had also nourished him. As much as he deplored hurting Joyce, he had felt loved and alive in the affair in a way he had never experienced before, and in a way he didn't want to live without in the future. It was an awakening.

Up until this point, Brian and Joyce had followed the conventional path into life they had learned as children. Both came from families with moderate means in the same small town. They married while working their way through college. After graduating, Brian worked like a demon. His passion for work was fertilized by a vision of liberating his family and children from the shame of a small-town past. He had been embarrassed in high school and college at not having the clothes, money, car, and other possessions his fellow students had. His ambition found traction in a medical supply company, where he was now executive vice president.

After college, Joyce worked for a few years and then quit to take care of their home and children. They stayed in their hometown because they wanted a sense of community that supported their family values. They admitted that they were proud of their accomplishments and wanted old friends, family, and others to see their success.

Brian and Joyce had devoted their lives to pursuing childhood values they had never questioned, yet neither of them had come to realize a life of their own. The affair broke the mold of their conventional behavior and brought them to a process of self-examination that wasn't concerned with "fixing" the marriage. The Jungian position is that becoming a mature individual is the foundation for participating in relationships, so most of the work was in individual sessions, though they met with me as a couple when we thought it would be helpful. Brian came to realize that he had been a prisoner of his past and that his passion to outgrow his early life had succeeded so well that he was left a successful man with no new channels for his hungry spirit. Likewise, Joyce recognized they had reached a plateau, where neither church nor society offered guidelines for growing further into a more personally satisfying life.

As their individual analysis progressed, they began to relate to each other more directly, honestly, authentically, and tenderly. As they grew individually, their relationship also grew. The purpose of meeting together with me began to give them a safe place in which to try out new aspects of themselves and to see how these aspects would affect their relationship. This transformation occurred over several years of careful, and often painful, analytic work. But the point to emphasize is that issues of sexuality broke up a stagnant, unconscious situation in order to *begin* a process of transformation, a renewal of the relationship between desire and soul in each of them.

This example illustrates the paradox of transformation. A life-shattering event, sparked by sexuality, became the impetus for the renewal of two lives on a higher level of wholeness. Sometimes, of course, lives are ruined and the relationship is lost. But regardless of the outcome, our psychological symptoms are trying to heal us, to transform us. As our work was nearing its end, Joyce said, "I almost think I should thank that damned woman."

The effects of this kind of work also spread throughout the circle of people whose lives we touch. Brian and Joyce's children learned to live with a new outlook based on a broader range of values, rather than become victims of their parents' emotional stagnation and toxic attitudes. Whenever we are transformed, it affects everyone around us.

Marriage is more than a legal document. It is a metaphor that expresses both cultural values and archetypal patterns as they come to life in human experience. In archetypal terms, marriage symbolizes the source of our creative selves, masculine and feminine, conscious and unconscious, feeling and thought, love and authority brought together through a desire for greater wholeness. In symbolic systems, such as mythology and alchemy, marriage represents the joining of opposites in order to birth something new, or to transform the level of consciousness. A deeper river of reality runs beneath all of our acts, giving them a meaning more compelling than we may realize. This doesn't mean we should stay in destructive marriages. It means we must work as hard as we can to discover the true meaning of transformation. If we don't, we may unknowingly take a course that is destructive to ourselves and to our society.

Cultural Transformation and Spirituality

The word "transformation" can be traced to the Latin *transformare*, which means to change the shape or form of something. Transformation does not mean revolution in the political sense, nor does it mean the mindless destruction of old values. It requires that we continue developing and refining the good that has been won throughout our lives and over the centuries. We force revolutions to happen only when we unconsciously hold fast to attitudes that are egocentric, stifling, and destructive. Such a calcified position eventually brings about a rebellion rather than a transformation.

The Garden of Eden story teaches us that all new growth in human consciousness begins with a necessary sin. The so-called sin is a step outside of conventional attitudes towards life. But if we are going to give our life to the Self—or to the image of the Divine within us or to any other transcendent value—we must first have our own life and personality to give. A personal life assures us that our actions and achievements disclose our true nature to others, whereas unconsciously following the conventional path means our behavior is involuntary. No matter how many proper things we do in the latter case, our life will reflect no unique personal or spiritual expression.

* * *

Before there was *The DaVinci Code,* Martin Scorsese in the late 1980s produced a film version of Nikos Kazantzakis's book *The Last Temptation of Christ.* Our entire country went into a state of shock—in the movie, Jesus had a sexual fantasy. Poor Nikos must have been spinning in his grave, because his novel had little to do with sex. Nikos Kazantzakis meant that Christ's last temptation was to become a successful upper-middle-class man, someone his mother, family, and community would be proud of.

While there is nothing wrong in being married and middle-class, it is the *spirit* of how we are living—whether we are conscious of what we are doing or not—that gives meaning to our life. We must ask ourselves if we have become free enough from our past to become a creative expression of our Self. The spiritual question that I believe challenges all of us is not "What do I do to be good?" but "How do I live to serve a value that is transcendent or Divine and can bring meaning into my life?"

Choosing to accept responsibility for our individuation, however, doesn't do away with our sense of freedom. Certainly it requires many sacrifices. But these sacrifices only affirm the tasks life has given us and can lead us beyond ourselves and into an authentic experience of meaning and fulfillment. Living with such authenticity can be difficult, for it brings us into continual collisions between our inner obligation to ourselves and our outer obligations to other people and society. It is as if authentic living, even when serving the Self, requires that we must always violate someone's idea of the "right" thing that we should be doing. But the more deeply we come to know ourselves, the more clearly we will experience what is "right" for us.

* * *

As Joyce and Brian reflected on the values that had been driving them away from their own authenticity, they discovered that their religious upbringing had compounded their problems rather than helping them become more authentic. They had been brought up to be good, kind, giving people who thought anger, depression, and even passion were dangerous emotions that should be avoided. The problem was not whether their values were right or wrong. They were too one-sided, stifling their imagination and creativity. In fact, Joyce and Brian were so afraid of anger and confrontation that they had lost their ability to communicate with each other.

We need relationships to continue our journey of growth. As Jung noted, "the unrelated human being lacks wholeness, for he can achieve wholeness only through the soul, and the soul cannot exist without its other side, which is always found in a 'You.'" That "you" can be another person or society. And while we must break free from the molds imposed upon us, we paradoxically need the other to help us grow and transform.

The Divine and the Individual

During my early religious life, God seemed distant and obscure. I was taught that he loved us, but I was never quite sure why. In addition, very little was said about the humanity of Jesus or the angry, tempestuous Yahweh, who seemed to fill the Old Testament. In short, neither God nor Christ were images of substance to me, and as a result, my spiritual image of myself lacked substance.

In my later years, I came across a line that the British psychiatrist R. D. Laing had written about relationships: "the person experiences not the absence of the other, but the absence of his own presence as other for the other." I believe this statement has a major impact on the psychology of parenting. It means it isn't how much we give our children, do for them, or even relate to them that gives them substance. It is how much they feel their importance to us, not to fill our emotional needs, but to be able to give something of worth to our lives.

If we are to have psychological and spiritual substance, we must know that our Self, God, or whatever image we have of the Divine, needs us in a vital way. It is as Jung suggested when he said that God seeks to fulfill his goal through the individual. Unconditional love may sound nice, but when given or accepted in an unconscious or shallow manner, it keeps the substance of the receiver from developing. I agree with Jung's position that God needs us for the fulfillment of creation as much as we need God for the fulfillment of our lives.

Yet there is an old heresy in the Christian tradition that counters this concept. This is the heresy of humility, or shame: that we are lost, no good, and need redeeming. This notion castrates our efforts to be spiritual, smothers our desires and devalues our souls. I have found that people who take this position frequently use it to cover secret feelings of righteousness, superiority, and even arrogance that they keep hidden in their shadow.

The word "humble" actually descends from the Latin, *humus*, meaning earth. To believe that being earthy or from the earth is worthless simply illustrates how far we have gone in devaluing nature. And it is our earthiness, our instinctual side, that houses our most basic source of desire. True humility is grounded in the earthiness of existence, which means that our spiritual quest is to fulfill our human nature, not to overcome or transcend it. The key to such fulfillment is realizing that through our own experiences of transformation we are participating in the ground of all being. These experiences encourage us to love life in its tragedy and its glory and to become an even stronger vessel for a love that can transform life for everyone who lives after us.

Love is more compelling than power, and once we open ourselves to transformation, it is desire, not law or fear, that moves us. The beauty of life draws us into it, and the invitation of the heart is stronger than the stern, impersonal requirements of duty. Likewise, transformation draws us toward it if we let it. And we will discover as we pass through the pain of life's contradictions that we will give birth to joy.

III. Transforming Lead into Gold

Questions for Reflection

- *What were some of the creative potentials you cut off to fit in as you grew up?*

- *What are some of the ways your repressed energy comes out?*

- *What is your wolf and how can you feed it?*

- *What kind of strangers scare you the most?*

- *Do you feel passionate about your life? What do you feel passionate about?*

- *What would you change to feel more fulfilled?*

- *What risks and sacrifices would you have to make?*

- *What parts of yourself do you keep hidden?*

- *Why do you think your own growth is important to our culture?*

Befriending Your Dreams

How are your dreams relating to your responses to your reading so far? What kinds of landscapes and moods have they been reflecting? As I noted, shadow figures often show up in our dreams as people who are the same sex as we are. What is the nature of some of the shadow figures showing up in your dreams?

PART
FOUR

The Wedding of Spirituality and Sexuality

In one transcendent moment of sexual union all of this can come
together and take fire, like the sun's light focused by a crystal.
From such a fire, we were given the gift of life. The invisible fire burns
with us as essence . . . . The fire burns in our loins and in our hearts.
We can exclude it from our consciousness, or we can tend it
and be warmed by it all through our lives.

—JUNE SINGER, THE POWER OF LOVE

Chapter 10

BODY AND SOUL

The body has its own way of knowing, a knowing that has little to do with logic, and much to do with truth, little to do with control, and much to do with division and analysis, and much to do with union.

— MARILYN SEWELL, CRIES OF THE SPIRIT

Nikos Kazantzakis opened his novel *Saint Francis* with a lovely prologue. In this prologue he described his personal connection with the essence of St. Francis's life as it flowed from the stream of Eternal Reality:

> I was overwhelmed by love, reverence, and admiration for Francis, the hero and great martyr. Often large teardrops smeared the manuscript; often a hand hovered before me in the air, a hand with an eternally renewed wound; someone seemed to have driven a nail through it, seemed to be driving a nail through it for all eternity. Everywhere around me as I wrote, I sensed the Saint's invisible presence; because for me Saint Francis is the model of the dutiful man, the man who by means of ceaseless, supremely cruel struggle succeeds in fulfilling our highest obligation, something higher even than morality or truth or beauty; the obligation to transubstantiate the matter which God entrusted us, and turn it into spirit.

As I read further into this passionate novel, I was surprised to discover that I was overcome not only with sadness but also with revulsion. In his writing Kazantzakis dramatically threw the spirit into a state of total warfare with the flesh, as he explained how St. Francis starved, beat, punished, and ignored his body in an effort to separate the spirit from the flesh (an idea that may have reflected Kazantzakis's perspective more than St. Francis's). As the novel progressed, the author vilified the flesh to such an extent with Saint Francis's intentional suffering that I could barely stand to continue reading. This view reminded me of my early religious education, whose purpose I came to think was to help me learn how to control and repress my sexuality, not to fully participate in it.

Our body is both the carrier of our instinctual nature, our basic source of desire, and the home of the soul and spirit during our lifetime. It is a serious error to believe that the body can be turned into spirit or made holy by punishing, belittling, or ignoring it. The body is made holy when we treat it as the carrier of the spirit created by the Divine.

As time left the Middle Ages and marched toward our present era, Western science began to follow a course that separated mind from matter. Since the age of Descartes, we have increasingly objectified our body and most of the natural world. When, as children, we begin to study health and biology in school, we find that our body is presented as an object in a drawing in textbooks. We learn that it is composed of various "systems" such as the nervous system, the digestive system, the circulatory system, and so on. Modern health-care delivery "systems" emphasize the mechanical view of these bodily systems, as if the body operates separately from the mind, emotions, and spirit. To take the example of medicine, fitness, and diet further, the underlying perspectives of our culture lead us to believe we can take charge of our body as though we are the project engineer on a job. Even New Age healing and spiritual practices, which consider themselves more "holistic" than mainstream medicine, also promote the idea that we can take charge of our health. As I work with people I'm often led to wonder if we have forgotten that we *are* our body. Have we forgotten that our sadness is reflected in the heaviness of our body, our joy in its lightness, our love in its excitement, and our denial or repression of our vitality in its rigidity?

We are our body, and at the same time we have the capacity to be in relationship with our body—listening to it, responding to it, caring for it, and even loving or hating it. In symbolic language, the body is the intermediary between humanity and the cosmos. Its changes depict the stages of life. The similarity between our bodies reflects our universality, and the fact that each body has distinct characteristics reflects our individuality. In Chinese medicine, the body is a dynamic force of interrelated functions corresponding to the elements of earth, wind, fire, and water, as well as to other symbolic categories. In astrology, the body as a whole is related to the symbolism of the Zodiac. In Christianity, the powerful image of the Last Supper depicts the act of giving the body as a giving of spirit.

Recalling the metaphor of alchemical transformation may help us to understand this relationship between various parts. Alchemy, as we saw, symbolizes the separation of the various ingredients of life and the recognition of the relationship that exists among them. This recognition leads to a reunification in which the new whole is more than the sum of its parts. As I have suggested, the process of transforming base metal into gold can be a metaphor for transforming ordinary life into sacred life, by separating and uniting the basic elements of our experience. Each such transformation becomes another step toward a truer value and meaning of life.

As we view the alchemical process through the eyes of mythos, we realize that we must become conscious of the spiritual aspects of the questions we encounter as we work with matter. Any symptom or state of dis-ease that we experience asks us how we need to change our view of ourselves, our world view, and how we are living. We must ask ourselves things like: Does my weight symbolize heaviness of heart? Does my anxiety mean my life is too pressured or my values too impersonal? or, Are my relationship problems trying to tell me I don't value my emotional life?

Whether great or small, these are spiritual questions. As the metaphor of the alchemical process continues, these questions will help us separate the elements involved—for example, in order for our self-awareness to grow, we may need to separate our vision of how we want things to be from the reality we face. And we must hold the tension generated until these elements move into conscious wholeness, in a new form that symbolizes a higher harmony. For example, as I said earlier, even after I had made a significant transformation I had to be willing to face the same process again. I had to accept the feeling that I had outgrown my "shell," even though my analyst and others couldn't see the reality of my position. I had to hold the tension between an inner feeling and outer skepticism. The dream image of the woman in the cell became a transforming symbol that moved me into a more passionate spirit of life.

We must consciously undertake the task of transforming life by infusing it with spirit, because flesh and spirit require each other to fulfill every level of life. And we must remember that we are the mediators between the profane and the sacred. We are part of creation but can also participate in new creation.

When we are devoted to our task, both the cycle of transformation—life, death, and renewal—and the tension of opposites are enacted within our psyche. There, as we grow spiritually and psychologically, we are transformed. When we fail to devote ourselves to this task, we experience the process of transformation internally as angst, or wounds to our soul—as Joyce and Brian experienced over Brian's affair, or the fear and revulsion Wendy felt whenever she encountered the bag lady outside her building. Externally, as in the situation of Katlin (the woman who discovered she didn't love her husband, Alan), we experience it as being stuck in a debilitating and disintegrating situation because of our inability to re-create ourselves on a new level.

Our society's sexual problems and difficulties reflect our collective fragmentation and need for renewal. However, sexuality also shows us symbolically the path toward healing. When we look at sexual desire in a more complex sense it is a force that seeks to renew life by uniting its separated aspects to produce new creative outcomes. Ken Wilber, author of over a dozen books and a scholar in the field of spirituality and consciousness, labels this reunification process the Path of Ascent. Wilber reminds us of Socrates' position that the Path of Ascent is driven by Eros and that as it progresses to greater and greater unions our personality will expand and deepen with each transformation.

Socrates asserted that lovers are taken out of themselves by Eros and enter into a larger union with the beloved, wedding their desire with soul. This path continues as we develop on higher and higher levels—from body to mind, to soul, and then to our origins—in Christian terminology, God.

Interestingly, the Hebrew word for knowledge, *da'at,* refers both to knowledge about life and to sexual knowledge. Symbolically, *da'at* suggests that we know something or someone so passionately and thoroughly that the outcome will create something new. In mythology this outcome is represented by the archetypal image of the child, an image that symbolizes fresh potentials in life. The outcome might be a new idea, an intellectual or artistic inspiration, or the beginning of a new relationship with a friend, lover, or some interior aspect of oneself. Like a child, the potential born into our lives must be carefully nurtured, mentored, and directed until it reaches maturity and can be integrated into our life.

* * *

After my divorce, it wasn't too long before I began to feel the pressure of desire working in my psyche. I was lonely and felt that there was a hole in my existence. I longed for companionship, intimacy, someone to share life and love with, but I was also scared. At the time I was still in graduate school, and it seemed natural to begin to research what love was all about. What happened, of course, as I sat in the middle of my life after divorce, trying to study my way out of my predicament, was that I found myself pierced by an arrow of desire that began to pull me out of the well of desolation that my childhood nightmare had left constantly available to me. I learned that I was capable of a kind of love I had never known before. The relationship ended badly, but suddenly I was awake and alive again. Still fearful, I had experienced a yearning that cries out for life. Though I was hurt deeply by its failure, I rejoiced because I knew I could feel passion and the quest for a greater life.

Once my desire had reawakened, it rapidly expanded across the horizon of my perception. I soon realized that Jung's point about individuation was that the world needs people who have come alive, who embrace risk and struggle to live—whose lives are a sacred task in which holiness is passion, and whose way to the Divine is through self-knowledge.

Once we're on this path, desire leads us into sexuality and love, a longing for a partner and a companion. But desire is not meant only to be satisfied. It is meant to grow and be refined without losing the instinctual urge from where it began, for this urge of the body is also an urge of the soul.

If we tend the fire and don't let it go out, it leads to a longer path. Desire is the compelling force that moves us toward unity—unity with another, with family, friends, and community, and ultimately with ourselves. As we move toward this unity, love continues to grow and progresses into compassion, a wider love of others. This path brings us full circle into the love of life, in both its sorrow and its glory.

What this line of thinking means to me is that my spiritual goal is to become fully alive. It is not to become free of desire. It is to have the freedom *to* desire. The spiritual writer John Eldredge says that we have only three options in today's world: "to be alive and thirsty, to be dead in our soul or to be addicted." I believe all of us truly want to be alive.

* * *

Remember that individuation relies on desire for motivating energy, and on values of the soul for meaning. As we consider these personal desires and values in the light of the values of our culture, we may see them begin to clash. And we must find a way to bring them into harmony, which may take a considerable amount of self-discipline. Mature self-discipline, which results from the development of self-knowledge, places the highest values of our heart in the forefront of our lives. It comes from listening to the murmurings of the voice within our soul, as reflected through the various aspects of our life. And it comes from holding the tension inherent in our conflicts—the tension between desire and duty, as well as between authenticity and conventional ideals. The long discipleship to self-knowledge teaches us the true relationship between ourselves and our surroundings: the symbolic way of the cross brings freedom from fear as it unites the profane and the sacred, bringing sexuality and spirituality into a dynamic harmony.

Sensuality and Soulfulness

We are created to be sensuous, and our sensuality is not only meant to be used in the service of instinctual procreation. In the Judaic and Christian traditions, God created this body—with skin to feel, with ears to hear, with a tongue to taste and speak, and with eyes to see. This living body brings to us the possibility of contact with the world and others, and also with ourselves and the Divine. At the heart of life is the sentient body, filled with the breath and the spirit of life, as the ancient word for both, *pneuma*, reminds us. The objectified body, seen as a machine, breathes only in the mechanical sense and loses its sensuality.

Love comes from the soul, through the Self, and infuses our physical being. We must be sensuous in order to experience love, whether with a lover, friend, or the Divine. Most saints believed that only a sensuous person could truly experience life and creation as sacred. Saint Teresa of Avila elegantly blends sensuality and spirituality when she speaks of her relationship to God by saying, "As a woman and a lover . . . I am moved by the sight of my Beloved. Where He is, I want to be. Where He suffers, I want to share. Who He is, I want to be: crucified by love."

Our troubles begin when we use our sexuality unconsciously, which we often do out of woundedness, ignorance, and fear. In my former marriage, sex became a battleground, as my wife and I each

159

fought to force the other person to fit an image of whom we wanted to love and how we wanted to be loved. I've known many people who have had such experiences. One was Gordon, who wanted his wife to love him unconditionally, which he believed included her having sex whenever he wanted. Another was Debbie, who wanted to swap sex for safety and reassurance, always keeping her partners frozen in a role of protector and mentor. And I remember Roberta, who felt so guilty about having sex, even with her husband of many years, that she couldn't allow herself to enjoy it.

These examples show us how easily we slip into using our sexuality in destructive ways. Imagine how Gordon's life might change if he could learn to enjoy his wife's love and sensuality in the way she enjoyed expressing it. Or how for Debbie, an intimate relationship might have a chance to grow if she learned to love herself. And imagine how Roberta's life might be different if she learned to believe her sensuality was a Divine gift.

Many of us seek sex to soothe our tired spots. Rick, for example, wanted sex for relaxation after a stressful day in the office. While sex can be renewing, it won't compensate very long for a life being lived at an unhealthy pace. Amanda had extramarital affairs for the sense of risk and adventure it brought back into her life at middle age. There are many people like Amanda, who want sex to stimulate empty lives and relationships, to distract them, or to make up the love they missed somewhere before. Sometimes we use sex in a quest for power, as a way of expressing rage at our inability to truly enter life and forge our identity. Sensuality, sexuality and love emanate from the soul. What we do with these gifts, how we respond to them and live them, determines whether they will come to life in a manner that is sacred or profane.

If we want our lives to be vital, gracious, and noble, we must learn to take love seriously. We must work for the consciousness that fertilizes love's growth and makes life sacred. But remember that we must also be compassionate with ourselves and allow ourselves to begin again. I used to think that woundedness was negative and a sign of failure. I was deeply ashamed to become the first person in my family to get divorced and then to have involved myself in a rebound romance that crashed. But woundedness is not a cause for shame or a reason to retreat from life. It is the first necessary step for spiritual growth and awakening. With a little courage to listen to our hearts, new desires will begin to stir us to seek healing and a bigger life.

Jung reminds us,

> Love is not cheap—let us therefore beware of cheapening it! All our bad qualities, our egotism, our cowardice, our worldly wisdom, our cupidity—all these would persuade us not to take love seriously. But love will reward us only when we do. I must even regard it as a misfortune that nowadays the sexual question is spoken of as something distinct from love. The two questions should not be separated, for when there is a sexual problem it can be solved only by love. Any other solution would be a harmful substitute. Sexuality dished out as sexuality is brutish; but sexuality as an expression of love is hallowed. Therefore, never ask what a man does, but how he does it. If he does it from love or in the spirit of love, then he serves a god; and whatever he may do is not ours to judge, for it is ennobled.

A Deeper Reality

It seems ironic that as we enter the twenty-first century we have to regain conscious awareness of the fact that sexual desire is numinous. Our society has tried so hard to reframe it into something simpler, like the right to personal pleasure or self-expression. Yet sexuality is not just a private matter. It joins us to the world and the stream of life.

What lamp must we hold to guide us in this area of intense unconscious darkness? I believe it must be the lamp of self-awareness, one that burns from a spiritual energy. If sexuality doesn't carry us into feeling love for what it joins us to, then we will continue on the path of disrespect, damage, loneliness and tragedy so prevalent in society today.

Our connection to our instincts is never theoretical. We must reflect upon the meaning of these matters as deeply as we can. Our "personal" or "private" relationships are, in fact, archetypal and affect all life. The way we live establishes the fundamental terms of our humanity; therefore, the way we love reflects the same.

Sexuality is the arena in which the heretic's challenge, the soul's challenge to our society is to be found. Issues related to sexuality—from the legitimacy of gay marriage to abuse cover-ups to dealing with pornography on the Internet—are challenging us to develop a new level of consciousness and spiritual maturity. We must grapple with these issues, not by seeking easy answers, but by holding them in a unity of tension as we explore them in detail, seeking the meaning behind them until we transcend them, transforming ourselves in the process. As part of this transforma-tion, we learn to recognize the significance of the stranger within ourselves and the stranger outside of ourselves. When we are open to strangers and greet them with ritual respect, they respond with extraordinary gifts. But when we fail to embrace them, we invite our own destruction.

Shock Waves

The wounds that manifest themselves through our sexuality often hit us like shock waves from an earthquake, because they go to the core of our self-esteem. They remind us that we are missing the purpose of life. If we remember that our sexual problems reflect our unconscious efforts to heal ourselves, they will show us the conflicts in which we are trapped.

From an archetypal perspective, our answers lie in the very heart of these conflicts. And one way to begin discovering these treasures is through the questions for reflection and dreamwork at the end of each part in this book. As we hold the tension, the pain of our dilemmas, and *seek to know the true questions* behind our predicaments, we must remember that a "return to normal" is never possible. What is called for is *transformation*, so we may evolve to a wholeness beyond what we've previously regarded as "healthy."

In fact, our penchant for the labels of "normal" and "healthy" is deeply mistaken. Our problems and difficulties in life do not make us dysfunctional or neurotic. We are only neurotic when unconscious of our problems; when we struggle to learn ourselves more deeply through our problems, we may suffer and encounter difficulty, but are not neurotic.

Every problem, Jung affirmed, brings an opportunity and a challenge, the possibility of a widening of consciousness along with the necessity of saying goodbye to childish trust in the habits of our youth. If, as we develop, we see the new problems life thrusts upon us as questions meant to deepen our understanding of life's meaning, they will increasingly provide us with opportunities to separate from the fake security of our conventional past. It's true that we often prefer quick fixes to long, patient work. But the gift of consciousness—that is, having the vocabulary, the resources to understand what our ancestors did not—should compel us to own and address what is wrong.

* * *

Life must be spiritual in order to be a pilgrimage. And the spiritual life has always asked for more than blind faith. It contains the guideposts that steer our life into being a pilgrimage of becoming, of expressing the soul's purpose for our life. These guideposts support the knowledge that a greater Reality exists than the one we see, and that we have a deep desire to relate to something greater than ourselves.

Unfortunately, the Western religious focus has been limited to how the spirit can help the body. But when the two work together, the body also offers help to the spirit. The seasons of the body's life, from birth through old age and to death, calls for the development of the spirit, and the dis-eases of the body can reflect and call attention to spirit's suffering. And as the life of the body declines, it challenges the life of the spirit to grow until the two processes join in the completion of a life.

Many of our spiritual and sexual difficulties come from our trying to deal separately with these aspects instead of realizing that they are part of a whole. In Christianity, Jesus was born into a common family to develop an ego identity as a carpenter, illustrating that the spiritual life begins by our becoming rooted in the world. In Judaism, Abraham became a man working for his father before he was called to his sacred quest. The Buddha similarly had to leave his princely home and become an ordinary man before he could begin his saintly life. All these examples show that the ability to bring one's own capacity for spirituality to full development depends on one's living life grounded in the body. After we take our place in society as a self-responsible person, we can then begin our journey into living more authentically.

As our pilgrimage on earth unfolds, we will begin to realize that the serious problems of life are never fully solved. In fact, Jung believed that if what we regard as problems *are* solved, this is a sign of our having lost their meaning, of our having become one-sided. The meaning and the purpose of our difficulties seem to be found in our untiring efforts to work on them and to learn to love this process, not in our ability to solve them. Every generation must relearn this truth. Our struggles to understand our problems and live into the questions they arouse, as Jung framed it, seems to be enough to "preserve us from stultification and petrification." This endeavor develops our consciousness, opens our hearts to new levels of becoming, and weds us fully to the experience of being alive.

Wholeness

Years ago I was anxious and controlling, even while desiring a life of freedom. But once I penetrated the surface realms of my humanity, I found myself more curious, more attentively open to the unexpected, and more aware of the importance of being with others.

There is an interconnectedness to all life—not life as an abstraction, but life as it is being lived through me—and you—in this very moment. As a desire for a fuller life has led me deeper into myself, I've begun to understand the underlying notion of wholeness claimed by all the great religions.

To feel the sense of wholeness supporting life is like coming home to ourselves. It is a moment of joy and serenity. And while it's a moment we can enjoy, it's not one we can hold on to. If we try, the effort will imprison us in the same way that never wanting to leave home can prevent our journey from continuing.

Desire may point the way to individuation, but it won't do my psychological work for me. Nor will desire bring me to a state where there is no growth or challenge left. But if I am open to the desire and religiously pursue my search for self-understanding, the potential for wholeness supporting me will always be close at hand.

Chapter 11

LOVE AND WHOLENESS

We can harness the energy of the winds, the seas, the sun.
But the day man learns to harness the energy of love,
that will be as important as the discovery of fire.

—Pierre Teilhard de Chardin, "A Song of Hope in a Changing World"

"Beauty and the Beast" was a challenging story for me during my younger years because it lacked the more familiar fairytale characters that I knew. Without a witch, a wicked stepmother, a wolf or even a frog, it seemed bleak. As a child the intuitive message I picked up was that if I was good, kind, and gentle, I would be loved and thereby be turned into a "prince"—that is, someone with a commanding presence who is appreciated and admired. During my midlife passage I took another look at this tale. From a psychological perspective, the Beast, who had initially seemed like an unfortunate, kindly fellow to me as a child, has a darker side to his personality. He demanded everything—the father's daughter and her complete devotion—all for the price of an eternally blooming rose.

This familiar story—in its original telling, and not its film incarnation—begins as a merchant father is leaving his three daughters for a long trip. Two of them ask for gifts of jewelry upon his return, but the youngest requests only a rose, a simple rose. On his way home the father is dismayed because it is winter and a rose is difficult to find. Eventually he sees a dark castle with its doors open, no one about and a large garden of blooming roses.

As the hapless merchant picks a small bud a monster instantly appears. The merchant begs for mercy, and the monster agrees to spare him on the condition that he will give up his daughter to become the Beast's bride. Back in the village, this lovely daughter enjoys the rose that never dies. But soon she has to keep her father's promise and go to live with the Beast.

The monster is kind, gentle, and generous with her. A few months pass and the girl misses her father so deeply that she feels compelled to visit him. The Beast cautions her that he will die if she fails to return to him, but the girl stays away a long time visiting her father. Finally she returns and finds the Beast dying in the rose garden. Moved to tears, she consents to marry him. At that point he is transformed into a prince; he had previously been turned into a beast by an evil witch.

This story shows how the simple desire for love, in contrast to other more worldly goods, begins our initiation into life. Life is like the beast; it is demanding and requires sacrifice and our full devotion if it is to become loving and transforming. It means that we must leave the safety of home, unconscious living, and the security of conventional values, or we run the risk of a dying life based on the safety of our past. The story reminds me of the many times that Joseph Campbell said we must learn "to live joyfully in the midst of the sorrows of the world." It also reminds me that if we embrace life with love, it never fades or withers and will reward us with a greater capacity for wholeness, wisdom, and compassion.

* * *

Many of us have become seekers because the beast of life wounded us early on through our family life or religious and social institutions. In some ways, we have become outsiders who failed to find a home in the conventional world. When my mother died in my childhood, I learned the importance of love by its sudden absence. Other people have had worse experiences. But when love fails us or vanishes and we no longer feel safe and at home in life, we are left wondering what we have done wrong to deserve such a fate. We are left stranded in a wilderness of the soul, and the journey out of this condition is a long one.

In my thirties, psychology promised me a new life. Humanistic psychology had become popular and one of its founders, Carl Rogers, focused it on *Becoming a Person,* the title of his major work. Other theorists added the importance of self-awareness and self-actualization. For the first time in mainstream psychology, woundedness was seen as necessary for growth and awakening from the dream of our barely lived lives. However, this point of view wasn't socially acceptable, and it didn't stay mainstream in psychology for long.

Shame kept me from seeking help for an awfully long time. Going to a therapist would have forced me to admit that something wasn't working in my life, and that I couldn't fix it. In addition, I knew in some subterranean place in my mind that this admission might carry with it a virus that could disrupt, even destroy, everything I had devoted myself to building. I had distracted myself by being busy, working hard, showing concern for my children, and saying to myself, "I've got everything a person could want. A business, family and good health." But deep inside I was unhappy, and I went for help when I couldn't deny my problems any longer.

Wounds cause us to be motivated by fear rather than a true desire for a richer life. In order to move toward an authentic life, we have to learn to deal with the beastly life we have encountered, the love we lost or never had, the unwept tears, the terror, the longings we shut down, or the prison we defensively have locked ourselves into. Therapy begins with slowly telling our story to a careful listener. This has the validating effect of helping us feel clearly understood.

Healing activates our intelligence and creativity. Once it begins, it forces us to choose whether we can now enjoy a regular life or will go on to desire more, a life open to our soul's desires. As C. G. Jung has taught me, we can each live a miraculous life, even turn our life into art. All we have to do is commit to the quest for self-knowledge. My journey, and the use of psychology as a means to understand it, has taught me that loving life, freedom and spiritual development depend on self-knowledge. Freedom requires that we have sufficient self-knowledge so that our deeds express who we are and are not controlled by the effects of wounds, childhood influences, and conventional values. Spiritual development further requires that, having achieved our freedom, we open ourselves to the inner voice of the Self. As it urges us to become, we will find a way to give love to the beastly face of life that is longing for transformation.

Desiring More

In the Middle Ages, our highest spiritual value was love, according to the great spiritual writer C. S. Lewis in his book *The Weight of Glory*. Since then, he tells us, we have turned our primary spiritual value from love to "unselfishness." This suggests that rather than securing a good life for ourselves and others, we should aim for the goal of self-denial.

Lewis explains that due to this, an idea lurks behind the scenes in our daily lives that to desire our own good and earnestly hope for it is a bad thing. He emphasizes that this idea is not part of the true Western spiritual tradition, nor is it the Christian idea of love. He then asserts that in reality our desires are not too strong, they are too weak. Simply put, we give ourselves away to busyness, acquisitiveness, and the pleasing of everyone but ourselves, instead of pursuing the fullness of life that is available to us.

Lewis knew that spirituality and sexuality have passionate histories in the Western spiritual traditions. The Nobel Laureate Elie Wiesel retells the legends of the Hasidic masters in a book entitled *Souls on Fire*, and another Nobel Laureate, Octavio Paz, writes of love and eroticism as *The Double Flame*. It is the fire of passion that drives both spirituality and sexuality and our desire for a truly rich life. When love enters the picture it becomes the field where both sexuality and spirituality can become humanized, personalized, transformed and creative. According to Carl Jung, love, when properly understood and lived, is more compelling than power, and once we open ourselves to transformation, it is attraction or desire, not rules or fear that will move us. The beauty of life will draw us into it, and the invitation of the heart will become stronger than the stern duties of the expectations thrust onto us by the world outside of ourselves.

We can have too much fire or not enough. Like love, the fire of passion and desire is helped, given direction and form, by self-awareness, insight, and understanding. This kind of consciousness, as I have explained, comes from our full participation in life and what we learn when we reflect on these experiences. The castle of the Beast, in other words, was dark until love became alive in it.

The writings of C. G. Jung provided me with the directions for living the kind of life Lewis suggests. They urged me to live a life that desires more abundance—not of material treasures, but of meaning, purpose, joy and love. Desire for a bigger life and the pursuit of self-knowledge helped refine my perception, and through this reflection, I could finally see the extraordinary path of my life before me.

We must return love to its rightful place as our highest spiritual value. Unless we are well on the path to self-knowledge, love remains a part of unconscious life, full of unresolved, unacknowledged fantasies, ideals, needs and hurts—the Beast in the fairy tale—and can be dangerous. Love without insight and understanding lacks form and direction. Sentimental love, for example, robs us of strength, certainty, and purpose. Romantic love becomes obsessive or compulsive. Sexual attraction may follow the same path, as what we think of as love may actually be an idealistic fantasy or the longing for security and emotional healing. Self-knowledge is the indispensable ingredient for authentic love to enrich our lives.

* * *

Four truths have become apparent to me in my own pursuit of self-knowledge as a way of life. First, I have learned that the fundamental assertion in most mystical traditions—that self-knowledge is the way to come to know the Divine—is absolutely true. Self-knowledge releases us from the prison of our personal history, de-conditions us from the attitudes of our parents and society, and forces us to work through our losses, hurts and grief. This act of purification, as the mystics called it, opens us to our depths, to the Self, the Divine energy within us.

The second truth I realized is that compassion must begin with myself. The cultivation of compassion toward my failures, shortcomings, and humanness opens the door to self-love and makes me a truly compassionate person with others. This process grounds us in our full humanity and supports the self-love implied in the commandment, "Love your neighbor as yourself." Self-love anchored in self-knowledge is the underpinning of how well we can give and receive love. Without self-love our structure of relationships will crumble under the pressure of the smallest storms, and our so-called unselfish acts will create an inner cauldron of resentment. I know this from the results of many years when I thought I could be hard on myself and loving to others. The only person I fooled was myself.

Self-love is like water flowing into a pond. When the pond is full, the water will overflow and begin to venture into the world. If we fail to know and love ourselves, we risk causing our souls to become arid and our hearts to stagnate in fear and defensiveness. What a wonderful paradox—loving ourselves is actually taking care of others.

The third thing I discovered is that a life based on the pursuit of self-knowledge continually takes us back into the world and among our communities. We cannot live a wholehearted life alone. We must participate in all the various relationships—attractions, love, friendships, conflicts, projections—to gain stimulation as well as the content that informs much of our search for self-knowledge.

The final thing that I gradually became aware of is that something inside me cares about me and my life. If I listen, it speaks to me through my dreams, fantasies, inspiration and thoughts. When I reflect, journal and work with my active imagination, it helps heal my wounds, turns my symptoms and failures into lessons, and aides me in discerning what my soul wants for my life. It does not save me from any of life's difficulties or catastrophes. But when I am suffering, it is there with me.

I have called this something the Self over the course of this book. As an analyst, I have studied and worked with the concept of the Self for many years. I've seen the validity of this concept by noting how it works in my life and in the lives of the people I counsel professionally. Today, I experience the Self very personally instead of viewing it from the distance of psychological theory. While I am not a theologian, I believe that my interactions with the Self are a true experience of feeling the love of the Divine.

The Self Seeking Incarnation

While struggling along in midlife, I realized that the better I knew myself the more my actions were my own and not those of the actor I had been trained to be. This helped me understand that, like our shadow, our ego is something we *have* and is simply part of our psyche. It isn't *who we are*, although it may feel that way. As part of our psyche, our ego has two purposes. The first is to give us an identity structure that enables us to live satisfactorily in the world. The second is to become the vehicle with which we discover our unfolding inner world, by bringing it into the light of consciousness.

As our development progresses, we will become more alive day by day, and our personality will continue to become or expand. We will become increasingly aware of who we really are, and of the Self seeking incarnation through us. As the ego and Self come into relationship, and our desire is wedded to our soul, the result is a unified personality, which makes living not only an art but also a sacred act.

The Jungian perspective is that as our unconscious contents are brought into consciousness, they themselves begin undergoing transformation. The potentials of sexual desire operate in much the same fashion. Sexuality teaches us to remember the beauty and the dangers of life. In its sublime form, it teaches us to catch a moment and to bring the beauty of it into full awareness. In its ominous form—especially in its neglected form—it will frighten and hurt us, reminding us that we have abandoned life's challenge to grow beyond ourselves.

Love and Wonder

In one of his essays, Rilke recalled the wonder he experienced upon reading Plato's great discourse on love, the *Symposium*, for the first time. Rilke says, "Surely there is much in the book. We do not grasp it yet; yet once upon a time it *was* grasped—who lost it? How did we spend the centuries? Where is he among us who dares speak of love?" When I was first divorced that is exactly what I wondered. How was it that sex could become a battleground? I didn't even want to think about it, much less consider re-entering the field of love and exposing myself to more hurt. I asked myself again and again how someone as successful and educated as I was had got into such a mess. Why hadn't someone taught me better or given me more preparation for these aspects of living?

I realize now that sexuality becomes a battleground when the vestiges of love die. In my early marriage, love had not been a romantic illusion; it had been the *psychological* illusion that to-gether we could grow up and find a place in life. The truth was, we were unable to grow together or even maintain a workable partnership, which left death or rebirth as the only options for the relationship. In this instance, death occurred after our attempts at rebirth had failed.

When working together, sexuality and spirituality can bring us vitality, passion and meaning. And the single container that can hold such a union is love, a basic theme in all of the great religious traditions, often in some form that is only imperfectly understood and certainly isn't simple. When not joined by love, either sexuality or spirituality can initiate a quest for power, which destroys the growth our nature compels us to seek. But when love forms the basis of our seeking, we have the passion to bring all our potentials into fruition.

* * *

People often ask me where to find the time for their reflections. We have to make the time. Remember, it has been common to all religious thought that seeking visions, insight, and Divine love requires that one go apart from the everyday world. When we allow ourselves to be caught in the sweeping tide of busyness, we soon end up experiencing our world as dull and ourselves as quite ordinary. It is only by stepping out of the everyday, even for a few minutes a day, that we can learn of the great events and love for life in store for us.

Another enemy of Divine love is the climate of fear that permeates the atmosphere of our daily lives. According to the anthropologist Loren Eisley, we fear the "ghosts of ourselves." This means the contaminated water, food, and air that have resulted from our heedless acts, or acts that yielded results we hadn't considered. We fear crime, terrorists, a world full of uncontrolled weapons, and the crush of a frantic lifestyle. We also fear being unable to afford food, shelter, and medical care. In other words, we fear for our safety in a way primitive people never did. Fear clouds our vision and dulls our senses. It makes us forget that the world longs to be seen through our eyes, listened to with our ears, and touched with our hands.

When I take my grandchildren to our local nature center, we begin our tour in a room designed for touch. First the things they touch are visible; then they put their hands into holes in a cabinet to identify what they are touching: bits of fur, bones, turtle shells, snake skin, and so on. Their eyes fill with wonder. The next room is dark and permeated with the sounds of nature in the wild. I hear these sounds mingling with their excited breath. The tour finishes with seeing live animals housed in natural habitats. The trip always awakens as much wonder in me as it does in them. It reminds me that we live in a world as astonishing as any fairy tale—a world made more for romance than for fear and busyness. I believe people of the world, whether city or countryside, are all wondrous in their own way.

In the context of spirituality and sexuality, love can breathe this perspective of wonder back into our lives. Love helps us see the pleasures of the body as our being unfolds toward wholeness over the course of a lifetime. Spirituality creates the sacred environment that makes our sexual experiences a safe place where we can abandon ourselves to the magic of wonder that union brings.

On the other hand, if we have dulled ourselves to the sensuous wonder of our hearts, the call to ecstasy is forced to come from the darker vestiges of our soul, through our shadow. Then drugs, less personal sexual activities, and stronger obsessions and addictions are sought in an effort break through our lifeless shell of existence. These are dangerous traps that eventually rob us of the sacred potential to experience love.

Love is identified with the sacred and the Divine in most of the major religions. The famous sculpture by Giovanni Bernini, *The Ecstasy of Saint Teresa*, magnificently shows the reclining ecstatic figure of the Saint about to be pierced by an arrow of love. In Teresa's face and body, Bernini clearly portrays Divine ecstasy as sexual ecstasy. He has captured in stone the Saint's own words:

> In his hands I saw a great golden spear, and at the iron tip there appeared to be a point of fire. This he plunged into my heart several times so that it penetrated to my entrails. When he pulled it out I felt that he took them with it, and left me utterly consumed by the great love of God. The pain was so severe that it made me utter several moans. The sweetness caused by this intense pain is so extreme that one cannot possibly wish it to cease, nor is one's soul content with anything but God. This is not a physical but a spiritual pain, though the body has some share in it—even a considerable share.

In the Roman Catholic nuptial liturgy we read, "Love is our origin, love is our constant calling, love is our fulfillment in heaven. The love of man and woman is made holy in the sacrament of matrimony and becomes the mirror of your everlasting love." Father

Andrew Greely says, "It is hard to think of that kind of love as sinful." And, I would add, it is hard to think of it as nonsexual.

In our world today, we also have to face the question of how spirituality can help form and guide other kinds of sexual relationships, such as those between gay and single people. We are all grappling with how to live in a new era where the models for how to be in a relationship are shifting. The old blueprint for a relationship was a plan that defined our roles and obligations for the rest of our lives. But our lives aren't that simple any more. One of the lessons we've learned in modern times is that the only constant in life is change. If we seek to learn how to face change and how spirituality can help form and guide our sexual relationships, the great religions tell us to approach these challenges from a position of love.

This perspective is clearly confirmed by the Apostle Paul, who presents love as the overwhelming answer to all questions and the fulfillment of all laws in First Corinthians. The Gospels support this assertion. In her studies of other great religious traditions, the scholar Karen Armstrong concludes that they all ask us to grow in spiritual consciousness to a place of compassion. This conclusion also defines the way we have to approach the great questions, such as nontraditional forms of love.

Yet even our religious institutions have, throughout history, often failed to keep this firm perspective of love and compassion at the center of the actions they support. We see this through the Inquisition, the sanctioning of wars, ethnic cleansings, and even the split in our society caused by fundamentalists. Without love and compassion, our moral nature becomes a stalking predator. When wonder and love are lost, our religious institutions likewise suffer.

Many religious traditions see Divine implications in the sexual act itself, which they view as a symbolic coming together of Divine forces. The Tantric tradition goes a step further and believes that sexual practices can be a means of obtaining spiritual perfection. These practices include ritual techniques and meditations through which the human couple is changed symbolically into the Divine pair Siva and Sakti. This is one of many spiritual traditions that seek to bring a sacred form to sexuality, and urge us to lend a broader definition to our connection to the Divine.

I wonder what it might be like to imagine, as Father Greely does in many of his writings, that the Divine is sensuous and loving. What if life longs for love, suffers and is beastly without love? The more we understand the relationship between sensual and spiritual, the easier this imagining becomes.

* * *

Sensuous feelings expressed through our touch, hearing, and taste open our sensitivity to ourselves. Our touch becomes more alive. Our hearing recognizes how important the words and sounds of love are. We become sensitive to our partner's every response through the exquisite varieties of contact and the warmth of closeness that can rise in intensity beyond our ability for words. We can grasp our partner's uniqueness while also feeling in these moments that he or she embodies the essence of the world. Through the other's humanness, we participate in the life force of the universe and our boundaries are pushed to their limits. Yet everything remains intensely personal as the center of our being is touched. It is infused with life energy until it can no longer contain it. Then orgasm explodes the shell of the personal, and we experience another dimension of consciousness. Our vibrating center becomes the center of the world—this is a spiritual experience.

But it doesn't have to stop there. By opening our senses to the wonder and beauty of the world, the spirit in matter becomes alive in everything. It is alive in nature, in what we eat, drink, wear and listen to. Living becomes an art. Sensitivity also teaches us that we must become selective and discriminating, learning to avoid things that offend, diminish and dull us. This may sound simplistic on paper, but it is actually a difficult approach to life. Yet this is a journey where desire doesn't stagnate, spirituality doesn't rigidify, and love doesn't become buried in sentimentality.

The Fire and the Rose

In the first chapter to this book, I noted that during my childhood despair I fled into the woods for solace and found a deeper Reality that would support and nurture me. Enfolded in this Reality, I felt the heartbeat of nature. This discovery marked my recognition of a grace beyond the understanding I had at that time. I needed decades of criticism, analysis, angry frustration, and reflection in order to find the metaphors in psychology and religion that opened the door to the experiential part of myself—the soul—the part within me where spirituality has its origins and finds its creative power. After all of those struggles, I arrived where I began in those woods and, as T. S. Eliot wrote, "[knew] the place for the first time." Jung summed up his own experience along these lines by saying, "I exist on a foundation of something I do not know. In spite of all uncertainties, I feel a solidity, underlying all existence and a continuity in my mode of being . . . ."

In adolescence, I was compelled, stumbling and terrified, onto the path of sexual desire that leads either to the soul's awakening or to an experience of life as a wasteland. But I had already felt the "hidden hand" supporting my existence and had seen, in my mother's illness, an example I couldn't yet accept of a love that conquers death. Love that comes from the soul's awakening through the journey initiated by desire, brought me a consciousness of death and a desire for life that was more powerful than my daily fears of risk and misfortune. The remedy has been effective and I remain in awe of it.

Love stretches from the beginning until the end of time—our personal time and all time. The foundation of life depends upon it. Through love we see everything, seeing into the mysteries of others and of life itself. Love is nourished by desire and desire is the creative force that represents all becoming. It begets the best of our aspirations and all higher consciousness.

Every generation has tried to name, picture, and describe "love," and yet for all of our efforts it seems someone before us has done so more beautifully. Jung noted that if we possess a "grain of wisdom" we will lay down our arms and name the mystery of love by the name of the greater mystery, God. This means that understanding love is a life's work that we cannot complete, though I believe the effort will greatly enrich us.

Love is the intensity of life and even conquers time, leading us beyond the everyday—even for a moment—and then returning us. And love touches every stage in our lives. Youth is thought of as a time of love, but when we look closer we see that it is actually a time of sex and fear—love must grow and mature as we do. And if we lose our capacity to love, we do so not because of age or illness, but because our soul has become arid and we have turned our back on life.

If we want to learn how to become fully human we have a long journey ahead of us. But I know from experience that this will be the most fulfilling journey of our lives. It may be fraught with pain and difficult transformations; but if we continue to pursue it, it will reveal to us a wonder and beauty previously unknown. Through love, we can forge the transcendent union between our sexuality and spirituality, the passionate place where the "fire and the rose are one."

IV. The Wedding of Spirituality and Sexuality

Questions for Reflection

- *How have you experienced the reawakening of desire?*

- *Describe the ways you experience your body as filled with the breath of life and spirit.*

- *How has this reading expanded the ways you can enjoy the sensual side of your life? Do any of these ways make you feel uncomfortable?*

- *Where do you find love in your life? By whom do you feel loved?*

- *How did you become a seeker? How long ago?*

- *Describe how you think your desires could be "too weak."*

- *How do these desires threaten you?*

- *What are your responses to the discussion of the Self as the Divine within us?*

- *What does it mean to you to have love as the place where the passions of sexuality and spirituality can come together?*

Befriending Your Dreams

As you've been reading, have your dreams been direct and fairly explicit, or are they more poetic? Can you see the story lines your dreams, the setting in which they begin, the unfolding of t action, and the setting in which they end? Do your dreams present a problem that reaches a solution, or do they trail off and end as you awaken? What are your dreams saying to you about love?

Appendix

At the end of each part in this book I have invited you to use two of the three techniques I described in the introduction as my spiritual practices. I call them my spiritual practices because I've learned that following them religiously continuously transforms my life for the better. They are journaling, as a means of reflection, befriending dreams, and active imagination. I am including two brief sections in this appendix that explain more about my approaches to journaling and dreamwork. I hope that you find them as helpful, exciting and transforming as I have.

Journaling Suggestions
from *Sacred Selfishness,* pp. 154–156

Important Elements in Personal Journal Writing

- Privacy insures trust and provides a space where we can encounter our many aspects truthfully.
- Self-understanding comes from writing down honestly who we are today within the context of our lives.
- Our journals become concrete records over time: studying them can reveal psychological patterns in our lives.
- Examining relationships, feelings, and interactions can be a source for discovering features of ourselves we have denied.
- Including our reflections in our personal journals leads to self-confrontation and to a new consciousness.

In our journals we should include our dreams and our thoughts and responses to them. As we're reflecting on the events we've recorded, we can write down any new insights, feelings, and other ideas or material that come to mind. A journal is also a good place to examine the feelings and behaviors we had during the day, or to the feelings we didn't get a chance to express.

Writing down a description of each situation where we think we feel a particular emotion can often help us get a better understanding of what's happening. For example, one man I know felt resentment whenever his wife suggested he might need a coat, a hat, an umbrella, or something else when he left the house. He thought she was treating him like a child. As he wrote about these situations he became aware that she might be expressing her care for him and he was "hearing her like a child" whose mother was chiding him. With this insight he was then able to accept and appreciate her love for him.

Journal keeping is both a personal workbook and an intensely personal form of self-expression. As such, it has no right or wrong format. All that matters is that you find a format that works for you, that fits your personality, and that can grow and change with you. Some people I know use elegant notebooks while others use a computer disk. I've always been the most comfortable with the kind of spiral notebooks I used in college.

Normal journaling takes about ten or fifteen minutes a day unless you're exploring something intensely. Then you may take longer, but rarely will you write for more than thirty minutes. People often ask me how they should handle dreams, and I advise them to write the dreams down immediately, whether it is during the night or first thing in the morning. Spouses, lovers, and other people in your home often have to learn to gracefully allow you some time with yourself before you start the day. In many circumstances, dreamwork attracts interest and the other people around you might start paying more attention to their own.

Journaling is a particularly good way of reflecting at the end of the day, and many people do it before going to sleep. The time of the day or the length of time you devote to journaling, however, can be worked out to fit your own pattern as long as you treat the practice with respect rather than as something you try to force into your schedule. You may take days off here and there to keep your journaling fresh, so that it does not become routine and mechanical. Your inner work has its own inner substance—this is the beginning, where you launch the journey deep within yourself.

Tips for Journal Writing

- Record what is going on or what has happened inside of you as well as outside.
- Make special note of strong emotional reactions during the day.
- Reflect on these reactions, and on the situations and relationships in which they occurred.
- Record thoughts, ideas, fantasies, and dreams.
- Try to simply reflect on dreams and see what they bring to mind.
- Record events that surround dreams and see if they seem related to you.
- Record drawings, poetry, quotations, and whatever else comes to mind.
- Record your personal fantasies and ambitions for both the present and the future.

In her foreword of her lovely and inspiring book *Gift from the Sea*, Anne Morrow Lindbergh explains how the book began as a journal "in order to think out my own particular pattern of living, my own individual balance of life, work and human relationships." She discovered through her writing, and talking about her writing with other people, that once she looked beneath the surface of life, many men and women in various circumstances and in many forms were "grappling with essentially the same questions." We are all seeking the sense of security that arrives when we have learned to become more intimate with ourselves. Journaling helps us find assurance that the creativity, values and ideals that arise inside of us are gifts we can nurture and develop. And when we have found out how to listen to ourselves we are able to act with strength, greet the world with joy, and share our gifts with others.

Dreams as Friends
from *Sacred Selfishness*, pp. 224–229

True friendship is both an art and a craft. Friendships may often seem to begin easily, but their nature is delicate at first; growth is slow and is easily checked or diverted. For friendships to become strong they need to be nurtured, cultivated and appreciated. Few of us are born with a natural gift for cultivating friendships. They take time, caring, and mutual respect. And the busyness that devours our lives makes enriching our friendships difficult. But once a friendship has become strong, it's very sturdy and reliable. A real friend can tell us things we don't want to tell ourselves, and yet we're always comforted to know there's someone out there we can lean on.

Some years ago the writer Sophie Loeb said, "A friend is one who withholds judgment no matter how long you have his unanswered letter." These characteristics of friendships explain why befriending the dream is an idea that makes immediate sense to most of us. It's much more comforting to feel that our inner lives are friendly toward us even if they're provoking us with dramatic images or confronting our preferred opinions.

In therapy it's tempting for both the therapist and the patient to translate dreams into their favorite theories, perspectives, or rationalizations. In many of these situations, dream interpretations are used to dredge up childhood conflicts; or to gain information, power, or energy from our unconscious to help us pursue our goals. Yet these approaches are actually hostile to our unconscious. They go against the grain of friendships, for nothing damages a friendship more than trying to exploit it. Unfortunately, modern therapies are often influenced by the social character of our times, which emphasizes solving problems in order to become more functional, rather than honoring our inner lives so that we can become more whole as human beings. When the fruits of friendship and the cultivation of our inner lives and wisdom aren't valued, therapy can actually work against our healing and growth and contribute to devaluing life.

The beauty of befriending dreams is that it doesn't require special knowledge and training. It simply asks that we *listen* to what they have to say to us and appreciate their importance.

Paying Attention

Paying attention to our dream lives involves several activities. To begin with, it's beneficial if we can create favorable conditions for receiving our dreams. An overextended schedule, exhaustion, poor sleeping habits, and the general habit of just being too busy can distract us from the quality time we commit to our dreams, or for that matter to any friendship. Making an effort to create an attitude of interest and receptivity by trying to have a good night's sleep and waking up gently very likely will invite a response from our unconscious.

The second way of paying attention to dreams is to write them down as soon as we wake up. It's better not to put them off until morning, if we remember them in the middle of the night, or to wait until after we've had coffee and are dressed. Time and experience have proven that until this friendship is firmly established, no matter how often we go over a dream in our minds, we can lose it in a moment if we haven't written it down.

Research proves we dream every night. If we don't remember the contents of our dreams, it usually means we're overtired, anxious, or have some other trouble keeping us from concentrating on our inner lives. Having a pencil and paper available nearby and writing dreams down quickly is a helpful ritual that stimulates our memory of them. When we wake up and don't remember a dream, lying quietly and focusing on what we have been thinking since we awakened can be helpful. Perhaps a thought or an image, a mood, an impression about ourselves in some past action, or thinking about the future will come to mind. Writing these thoughts down can revive or recall others, jump-starting a train of thinking that can lead to reconstructing a dream.

I've often awakened in the morning and been surprised by the number of dreams I wrote down during the night with no memory of even writing them. At other times, when I only recall a brief scene, I've discovered that writing it down carefully may help the entire dream return to memory. A short time ago I remembered the image of a brown bear from a dream. As I was writing a detailed description of the bear, the dream story began returning and eventually covered three pages.

And now we come to the third important aspect of paying attention to a dream, which is to write it down with all the detail you can. Recording it carefully helps you to see or feel the full development of the dream. And describing the moods, people, animals, landscapes and actions in lively ways helps you reimagine the dream as a story that you can experience again.

In his delightful and wise book *The Star Thrower*, anthropologist Loren Eisley shares a dream in a manner that pulls us directly into it:

> The dream was of a great blurred bearlike shape emerging from the snow against the window. It pounded on the glass and beckoned importunately toward the forest. I caught the urgency of a message as uncouth and indecipherable as the shape of its huge bearer in the snow. In the immense terror of my dream I struggled against the import of that message as I struggled also to resist the impatient pounding of the frost-enveloped beast at the window.
>
> Suddenly I lifted the telephone beside my bed, and through the receiver came a message miraculous in origin. For I knew intuitively, in the still snowfall of my dream, that the voice I heard, a long way off, was my own voice in childhood. Pure and sweet, incredibly refined and beautiful beyond the things of earth, yet somehow inexorable and not to be stayed, the voice was already terminating its messages. "I am sorry to have troubled you," the clear faint syllables of the child persisted. They seemed to come across a thinning wire that lengthened far away into the years of my past. "I am sorry, I am sorry to have troubled you at all." The voice faded before I could speak. I was awake now, trembling in the cold.

As I read this dream I feel like I do when I read a good poem—left with a sense of wonder. Most of us have to relearn how to express ourselves in such a complete manner.

Julia Cameron, in *The Right to Write*, offers useful advice in this direction by urging us to become what she calls "bad writers." By this phrase she means letting everything be expressed even if we think we're describing feelings and events in tabloid terms, where beauties are breathtaking, villains hideous, victims helpless, and murders grisly. We've been so schooled to censor ourselves, putting down "just the facts." When we do this we can end up losing the poetry and flavor of our dreams, like someone who stops digging in a hollow tree a few inches before reaching the honey.

Listening

Listening to the dream includes writing it down as completely as we remember it and including its colorful aspects. However, we must keep in mind that listening to a dream is similar to what we do when we *really* want someone to listen to us: We want them to put their agendas, their censoring mind-sets, and their "plans" to answer us aside. This is why I like to tell people that while writing the dream down, they should suspend the temptation to interpret it. Likewise, if we're thinking of dream theories and interpretations or problems in our lives, we can't be fully listening to the dream and are in danger of forcing it into a framework we already have in mind. I once heard someone say that we don't need to kill the bird in order to study it; it's much better to let it sing—and the same is true with dreams.

A second aspect of listening to dreams is also made possible by writing them down—sooner or later we'll have collections of them we can review as a dream series. These series are like ongoing conversations with our unconscious, the structure that supports our lives. One of my clients reviewed his dreams over a period of several months. He first read over them to get a feeling of their different emotional contents. Then he made a list of the main characters and their positive and negative attributes, a list of the places where the dreams took place, and a summary of their story lines and outcomes. He discovered that many of the dreams seemed to fit in the series like chapters in a larger story and his feelings in them appeared like nuances of color in a large painting. This activity can be fun as well as offering important insights into how we're growing and changing, and how some of our dearly held attitudes and beliefs are being consigned to the past.

Questioning

The questions we ask ourselves about our dreams can fall into as many areas as we can imagine. Just as examining a painting reveals its details and beauty, questioning a dream opens up the view of specific scenarios and leaves us wondering where is this place, who are these people, what are they like, why do they keep appearing? We may ask ourselves why this animal, this landscape, this concern or this dream is appearing in our lives at this particular moment. The unconscious is trying to tell us where our energy is, and where it's going, in the plot or story line of the dream. With this in mind, it becomes important to ask how the dream is developing and how it is concluding.

Reflecting

Reflecting on our dreams can be like selecting new clothes. We have to try them on, and if they seem to fit, we take them. Then we have to wear them for a while and move around in them until they feel comfortable. Similarly, we may mull over a dream's images and moods and consider the questions we've asked and the answers that come to mind as we're trying to figure out how the dream "fits." Finally the dream's components may become part of our lives and change our habitual way of seeing things, especially ourselves. In other words each little bit of new understanding we gain is something we integrate in a manner that expands our awareness.

Bibliography

Armstrong, K. 2001. *The Battle for God.* New York: Ballantine.

Bly, R. 1995. *The Soul Is Here for Its Own Joy.* Hopewell, N.J.: Ecco.

Burkert, W. 1985. *Greek Religion.* Cambridge, Mass.: Harvard University Press.

Cameron, J. 1998. *The Right to Write.* New York: Tarcher.

Campbell, J. 1949. *The Hero with a Thousand Faces.* Princeton, N.J.: Bollingen Series.

Campbell, J., with B. Moyers. 1988. *The Power of Myth.* New York: Doubleday.

Camus, A. 2004. *The Stranger.* London: Cambridge University Press.

Combs, A. 1995. *The Radiance of Being: Complexity, Chaos, and the Evolution of Consciousness.* Edinburgh: Floris.

Conroy, P. 2003. *My Losing Season.* New York: Dial.

Culbertson, P. L. 1995. *A Word Fitly Spoken.* New York: SUNY Press.

Dalley, S. 1998. *Myths from Mesopotamia: Creation, The Food, Gilgamesh, and Others.* New York: Oxford University Press.

Dostoevsky, F. 2002. *The Brothers Karamazov.* New York: Farrar, Straus and Giroux.

Edinger, E. F. 1972. *Ego and Archetype.* New York: Putnam.

_____. 1985. *Anatomy of the Psyche: Alchemical Symbolism in Psychotherapy.* Chicago: Open Court.

Eisley, L. 1979. *The Star Thrower.* New York: Harvest.

Eldredge, J. 2001. *The Journey of Desire*. Nashville: Nelson.

Eliade, M. 1968. *The Sacred and the Profane*. New York: Harvest.

———. 1987. *Encyclopedia of Religion*. New York: Macmillan.

Eliot, T. S. 1971. *Four Quartets*. New York: Harcourt, Brace and Co.

Fox, E., trans. 2000. *The Five Books of Moses*. New York: Schocken.

Freedman, D. N., ed. 1992. *The Anchor Bible Dictionary*. New York: Doubleday.

Freud, S. 1943. *A General Introduction to Psychoanalysis*. J. Riviere, trans. New York: Garden City.

Fromm, E. 2005. *To Have or To Be?* New York: Continuum.

Godwin, G. 1999. *The Finishing School*. New York: Ballantine.

Greeley, A. M., and J. Neusner. 1990. *The Bible and Us: A Priest and a Rabbi Read Scripture Together*. New York: Warner.

Grimm, J., W. Grimm, and J. Scharl. 1976. *The Complete Grimm's Fairy Tales*. New York: Pantheon.

Hannah, B. 1991. *Jung: His Life and Work*. Boston: Shambhala.

Harris, C. T. B. 2002. *Sacred Selfishness: A Guide to Living a Life of Substance*. Maui: Inner Ocean.

———. 1995. *Emasculation of the Unicorn*. Maine: Nicolas-Hays.

Harris, M., and C. T. B. Harris. 1996. *Like Gold Through Fire: Understanding the Transforming Power of Suffering*. Philadelphia: Xlibris.

Hillman, J. 1967. *Insearch: Psychology and Religion*. Revised edition. New York: Spring Publications, 1994.

Homer. *The Iliad*. R. Fitzgerald, trans. New York: Farrar, Straus and Giroux, 2004.

_____. *The Odyssey.* R. Fitzgerald, trans. New York: Farrar, Straus and Giroux, 1998.

Jacobi, J. 1983. *The Way of Individuation.* New York: Meridian.

James, W. 1999. *Varieties of Religious Experiences.* New York: Modern Library.

Jung, C. G. 1954. *The Collected Works.* R. F. C. Hull, trans. H. Read, M. Fordham, G. Adler, and W. McGuire. eds. Princeton, N.J.: Princeton University Press.

_____. 1961. *Memories, Dreams, Reflections.* A. Jaffe, ed. R. Winston and C. Winston, trans. New York: Pantheon.

Jung, C. G., ed. 1978. *Man and His Symbols.* New York: Picador.

Kazantzakis, N. 1962. *Saint Francis.* P. A. Bein, trans. New York: Simon and Schuster.

Kluger, Y., and N. Kluger-Nash. 1999. *A Psychological Interpretation of Ruth.* Zürich: Daimon.

Küng, H. 1984. *On Being a Christian.* New York: Doubleday.

Laing, R. D. 1971. *Self and Others.* Second edition. Harmondsworth, England: Penguin.

Lewis, C. S. 2001. *The Weight of Glory.* San Francisco: Harper.

Lindbergh, A. M. 1986. *Gift from the Sea.* New York: Pantheon.

Lockhart, R. 1963. *Words as Eggs.* Dallas: Spring Publications.

Luke, H. M. 1992. *Kaleidoscope.* New York: Parabola Books.

May, R. 1969. *Love and Will.* New York: Dell.

Meir, C. H. 1977. *Personality.* D. N. Roscoe, trans. Switzerland: Daimon.

Merton, T. 1953. *The Sign of Jonah*. New York: Harcourt Brace.

Mitterrand, F., and E. Wiesel. 1996. *Memoir in Two Voices*. New York: Arcade.

Morford, M. P. O., and R. Lenardon. 1985. *Classical Mythology*. New York: Longman.

Otto, R., and J. M. Harvey. 1958. *The Idea of the Holy*. New York: Oxford University Press.

Palmer, P. "In the Belly of Paradox." *Pendle Hill Pamphlet 224*, Pendle Hill, Penn.

Paz, O. 1996. *The Double Flame: Love and Eroticism*. New York: Harvest.

Price, R. 2003. *A Whole New Life: An Illness and a Healing*. New York: Scribner.

Rhodes, J. M. 1924. *The Apocryphal New Testament*. Oxford: Oxford University Press.

Rhodes, L. 2000. *Into the Dark for Gold*. San Francisco: Science and Behavior.

Rilke, R. M. 1975. *Rilke on Love and Other Difficulties*. J. J. Mood, trans. New York: Norton.

_____. 2002. *Letters to a Young Poet*. New York: Dover.

Sanford, J. A. 1987. *The Kingdom Within: The Inner Meanings of Jesus' Sayings*. San Francisco: Harper.

Teresa, St., of Avila. *Interior Castle*. E. A. Peers, trans. New York: Image.

Tolstoy, L. 2003. *The Death of Ivan Illyich and Other Stories*. New York: Signet Classics.

Underhill, E. 1999. *Mysticism: The Nature and Development of Spiritual Consciousness*. Oxford: One World.

van der Post, L. 1953. *The Face Beside the Fire.* New York: William Morrow.

Wiesel, E. 1994. *From the Kingdom of Memory.* New York: Schocken.

Wilber, K. 1995. "The Way Up Is the Way Down." *Parabola* XX(4).

Wolfe, T. 1995. *Look Homeward, Angel.* New York: Scribner.

_____. 1998. *You Can't Go Home Again.* New York: Harper Perennial.

Yeats, W. B., ed. 1988. *A Treasury of Irish Myth, Legend and Folklore.* New York: Gramercy

Index

Abraham, 98–99, 109, 125
Ackerman, Diane, 1
active imagination, 94, 183
Adam and Eve, story of, 101–2,
    126, 128
addiction, 26
alchemy, 90, 129–30, 135,
    146, 155
Alcoholics Anonymous, 115
alter ego, 54
ambition, 53
anti-Semitism, 113
Aphrodite, 7, 20, 23, 55
apple, as symbol, 127–28
archetypal concepts, 94
archetypal patterns, 54, 93, 101
archetypal truth, 127
Ares, 7
Armstrong, Karen, 66–68, 176
astrology, 155
Athena, 55
authenticity, 147–48, 159

Beauty and the Beast, 166
Bernini, Giovanni, 175
Bhagavad Gita, 58
Bible, 32, 67, 92, 102 (*see also* Old
    Testament, New Testament)
body, 154–55, 159, 163–64, 175, 180
Bohr, Niels, 87
breath, as an image of the spirit, 31
Buddha, 12, 58, 67, 100, 134, 164
Buddhism, xvi

Cameron, Julia, 189
Campbell, Joseph, 36, 54–55, 100,
    131, 167
Camus, Albert, 108–9, 125–26
caves, at Lascaux, 47
celibacy, 143
Christ, 67, 134–35, 147–48
Christianity, xvi, 47, 133, 155, 164
Cole, Thomas, 136
compassion, 171, 176
complexes, psychological, 44
complexio oppositorium, 89
Conroy, Pat, 126
consciousness, 65
conservatism, 133
Cronus, 20
cross, as metaphor or symbol,
    134–35, 159

dark night of the soul, 132, 135
death, 45, 48, 54–55, 72, 66, 72, 95,
    101, 109, 115, 126, 132, 138–39,
    178; longing for, 33
depression, 90–91, 100
depth psychology, 67
Descartes, 154
desire, xi–xii, xiv, xvi, 35–36, 55,
    57, 95, 100, 102, 116, 123–24,
    127, 139–42, 145, 149, 154,
    157–59, 165, 169–70, 172, 178,
    180; sexual, 7, 11, 16, 34, 100,
    120–21, 141, 143, 156, 161, 172;
    spiritual, 16

Inanna, 54
individuation, xix, 43, 46, 86,
    128, 130–31, 134–35, 147, 158,
    165
infidelity, 142
instinct, 47, 80, 90, 102, 162
Interpersonal Psychiatry, 112
Isaiah, 85
Ishtar, 54

Jacob, 109
Jacobi, Jolande, 114
James, William, 60
Jesus, 58, 135, 147–48, 164
Job, Book of, 28–29
Jonah, 81–82, 100
journaling/journal keeping, xii–xiii,
    73, 183–85
Judaism, xvi, 127
Jung, C. G., xiv, xviii, 18, 26–27, 29,
    36–38, 41, 43, 45–46, 54, 64–65,
    79, 84, 88–89, 114, 117, 128–30,
    138, 148–49, 158, 161, 163–64,
    168–70, 178
Jungian analysis, 86, 94, 132
Jungian psychology, xv, 26, 33, 37,
    46, 61, 68–69, 85, 94, 129

Kazantzakis, Nikos, 147, 153–54
Keats, John, 3
Kluger-Nash, Nomi, 99
knowing, 27–29 (see also self-
    knowledge)
Krishna, 58
Küng, Hans, 134–35
Laing, R. D., 148
language, 13, 32, 56
Lewis, C. S., 169–70

life, 66, 72, 87
Lindbergh, Anne Morrow, 185
Loeb, Sophie, 186
logos, 66–68, 125
love, xiv, xix, 14, 16–17, 26–27, 34,
    48, 55–57, 60, 77–80, 82, 88–89,
    97, 102, 119, 125, 127, 143,
    149, 157–61, 167, 170–71, 173,
    175–81; and eroticism, 169; and
    sex, 22–23, 26 (see also sexuality);
    as a foundation for a satisfying
    life, xiii; as a spiritual value, 169;
    God's (Divine), 128, 172, 174;
    nontraditional forms, 176

mandala, 41, 43, 45
marriage, 143, 145–46
    gay, 162
Mary, 58
May, Rollo, 77
meaning, 56–57, 62, 64, 67–68
medicine, Chinese, 155
Merton, Thomas, 80, 82, 85–87, 92
metaphor, xviii, 7–8, 67, 92–96, 98,
    100–103, 123–24, 129–30, 146
midlife, 83–84, 131, 139
midlife crisis, 39, 45, 100
militia movement, 117
mind, and matter, 154
monotheism, 133
Moore, Robert, 64
Moses, 58, 67, 99, 124
multiculturalism, 10
multiple personality disorder, 119
mysticism, 15; Christian, 115
mystics, 68
myth/mythology, 68, 94, 101, 109,
    122, 133, 146, 157; ancient, 129;

Bud Harris, Ph.D., is a certified Jungian analyst, a graduate of the C. G. Jung Institute in Zürich, Switzerland. He received his doctoral degree in counseling psychology from Georgia State University in Atlanta, Georgia. Bud combines over fifteen years of business experience with over thirty years as a practicing psychotherapist, psychologist and Jungian analyst, bringing practicality and depth to his work. He has lectured widely and written a number of articles and books. He currently lives and practices in Asheville, North Carolina.

More information is available about Dr. Harris on his Web site, www.budharris.com, where you may also sign up for his quarterly newsletter.